THE BEAUTY OF
BRITAIN

THE BEAUTY OF
BRITAIN

Foreword by
The Marquess of Salisbury

Edmund Swinglehurst

British Heritage Press

Photographic acknowledgments

All photographs in this book are by Colour Library International, London, with the exception of the following: Catherine Blackie, London, pages 42, 91; W. F. Davidson, Penrith, pages 152, 154–5; Michael Dent, East Twickenham, pages 24, 48, 198 top; John Green, London, pages 10, 62, 64, 157, 198 bottom, 199; Angelo Hornak, London, page 15 right; Susan Lund, Prestwood, pages 13, 89, 163 bottom; Pat Pierce, Sunbury, pages 18, 22; Judy Todd, London, pages 23, 25, 54, 90, 94, 97 bottom, 106, 124, 127, 137, 140 top and bottom, 146 148, 158, 200, 208, 209 top, 218, 237, 242, 243.

Front cover: Cavendish, Suffolk (Tony Stone Associates).
Back cover: Loch Garry, Highland Region (Colour Library International).
Endpapers: Ullswater, Cumbria (Colour Library International).
Title page: Aylesford, Kent (Colour Library International).
Foreword: Hatfield House, Hertfordshire (Tony Stone Associates).

Copyright © The Hamlyn Publishing Group Limited 1983

First English edition published by
Dean's International Publishing
A division of The Hamlyn Publishing Group Limited
London · New York · Sydney · Toronto
Astronaut House, Feltham, Middlesex, England

This 1983 edition published by British Heritage Press
Distributed by Crown Publishers, Inc.
Library of Congress Catalog Number: 83-70 131
ISBN 0-517-410184
h g f e d c b a

Printed and bound by Graficromo s.a., Cordoba, Spain

Contents

Foreword

Shakespeare in his incomparable language eulogised this Sceptred Isle and the people who inhabited it. Many have followed his lead though few have equalled the beauty of his language. He gave high praise to its peoples, who built so successfully on what Nature had endowed them with, adding with a sure touch to the canvas provided for them by Nature.

Perhaps nowhere else in the world is there such a diversity of beauty in so small a space. Some of it is Nature's work alone, such as the wild highlands of Scotland, Wales and the Lake District and the rugged coastline. Some is in part natural, such as the rolling farmlands on which man has superimposed the patchwork of fields and farms. Some is Man's: the great cathedrals, the ancient towns, the country houses and manors. It has all blended successfully into a cohesive whole on which, over the years, time has spread a gentle patina. Its people take pride in their inheritance and value it and wish to conserve it, even though the cost of doing so is high. But at the same time, they are active and creative and have kept abreast of modern developments in an ever-changing world. Life continues at an increasing tempo, whether in the countryside, the bustling towns and cities or the factories on which the life blood of the country depends.

Since Shakespeare's day there have been many who have carried the torch which he set alight. This magnificent book is the latest. The splendid photographs, of the highest standard, give a broad picture of the various aspects of our islands. They are accompanied by an elegant text which complements the illustrations and enlarges on them.

It is surely a book which will give enormous pleasure and one to which the reader will return again and again with renewed enjoyment.

Salisbury

The British Enigma

Travelling about Britain, one sometimes has the feeling that the whole country has been landscaped by a titanic Capability Brown. The checkerboard of fields that spreads from the fringe of southern cliffs and stretches away in all directions has an inventive pattern of shapes that change with every contour. Here and there, the pattern is punctuated by the dark patch of a copse, or broken by the arabesques of rivers gleaming between tree-crowded banks. For contrast, there are bare areas of moorland and heath, for drama an escarpment or a sudden hill crowned with woods, for surprise a secret gorge, or a lake buried among hills.

Much of the British countryside is man-made, its shape dictated by the tides of history. Commonland, enclosures, forests, parks, roads and paths all reflect compromises between the rights of kings and barons, squires and peasants, landlords and tenants and government and public. There is hardly a foot of the British countryside that, told in terms of its significance as history, law, agriculture, sociology, botany or zoology, could not be written about at length.

In this basic setting, built over the centuries, there are also the man-made decorative elements and the wastelands. A viaduct by Thomas Telford streams across a green valley like something in an eighteenth-century *trompe l'oeil* painting; cathedrals rise out of clusters of diminutive cottages; castles stand like toy forts on hilltops or in the bends of rivers; a jumble of miners' houses huddle among the slag heaps; and a brave new world is reflected from the vast metal bowls of modern technology looking as strange as a modern Stonehenge on the cliffs of Devon and Caithness.

The contrasts of the British landscape are an expression of the character of its people. Conventional and conformist at first sight, but full of infinite variety on better acquaintance. It is not for nothing that eccentricity has always been regarded as something to be proud of, but in a typically British way with an air of apology. 'Being different' from the conventional is not outwardly encouraged, but it is secretly respected.

These differences in the character of countryside and people arise out of the nature of the land itself as much as from accident. People who have struggled with the hard environment of the Highlands, the Pennines, or the Cumbrian Mountains, are inevitably different from those brought up in the lush meadows and parklands of Hampshire and Wiltshire. So too, the dark and sturdy Iberian is different from the Celt, and the Anglo-Saxon from the more sophisticated Norman who arrived in 1066 and imposed the idea of a unity which has been woven so firmly into the fabric of the country that none of its inhabitants is consciously aware of it. In fact, most people preserve the idea of their divergence. North of the border the Scot regards himself as an entirely different person from the 'Sassenach' to the south, and the Welsh are continually campaigning for more education and entertainment in the Welsh language. In England the Yorkshireman does not like to be confused with a man from Lancashire, and in Kent there is a dividing line between Kentish men and men of Kent.

Little wonder that the world hardly knows what to make of the British who, from owning the world's largest empire, can slip quite casually and relatively unperturbed into the role of least successful of the industrialized nations.

Historically, it has always been thus. In Tudor times, now regarded with nostalgic sentiment as the golden time of bluff King Hal and good Queen Bess, England was small fry to the Continental powers. In the seventeenth century, Louis XIV, the 'Sun King', hardly bothered to let his glorious rays fall on England's ambassadors, though the revolutionaries of 1789 and after had a high regard for English thought. Napoleon and Hitler both underestimated the 'nation of shopkeepers'; today most people think the British underestimate themselves.

The answer to the enigma of this perplexing island nation is in the country itself, in the contrasts and liberties which its underlying unity allows it to indulge in, and permits thought to range freely and new solutions to the problems of society to be formulated.

In setting out the structure of this book we have tried as far as possible to group the essential areas of historical, social and topographical unity together. We hope in this way that the traveller in Britain will become aware of all the facets of the complex personality developed by a nation with one of the longest continuous threads of civilization in the world.

Preceding page: Rhuddlan Castle is near Rhyl in north Wales. The castle is protected on three sides by a moat and on the fourth by the River Clwyd. James of St. George completed the building of the castle, a fine example of the concentric type, in 1282.

Below: The Cuillin Mountains, beloved by walkers and mountaineers, rise on the deeply indented west coast of Skye. The highest peak is Sgurr Alasdair (3,309 ft/1009 m). This view is from the Sleat Peninsula across Loch Eishort.

England

London – The Great Metropolis

'Maybe it's because I'm a Londoner', goes the song, 'that I love London Town.' But who is a Londoner? He used to be the Cockney born within the sound of the bells of Bow Church in the City of London. But now he comes from a polyglot population made up of English, Irish, Scottish and Welsh, Australian, Asian, African, Arab, West Indian and a sprinkling of most of the nations of the earth. In addition, there are some fourteen million honorary Londoners who take up temporary residence in the metropolis, mostly during the summer months. They have come for the Trooping the Colour ceremony, the Tower of London and the shops along Oxford Street, but when they depart they leave something of themselves behind.

This multiplicity of races mingling in London's centre and sometimes concentrated in particular suburban areas – Asians in Southall, West Indians and Africans in Brixton, Cypriots in Camden Town, Arabs in Earls Court (it used to be Australians in 'Kangaroo Valley', but they have moved on, many to Hampstead and Highgate) – is not a new phenomenon. London has many times welcomed people who have wanted or have been obliged to leave their native land. French Huguenots came to London's East End and so did refugees from the 1789 Revolution; Armenians arrived in the nineteenth century, and Austrian and German Jews, including Karl Marx, in the nineteenth and twentieth, and all of them gradually integrated with the population, only their names revealing their origins. The changing population has given a new life to many parts of the ancient city, and districts have become more colourful, with shops and restaurants reflecting indigenous tastes and festivals expressing the different cultures.

If new attitudes have changed London's atmosphere, then new architecture has changed its face. Many fine old buildings, the heritage of a remarkable historical development, still remain, but now there are new forms and designs rising above the Gothic (mostly Victorian) spires, Renaissance-style towers and elegant Georgian terraces. The new architecture may not please everyone, but there is no doubt that it offers new and sometimes surprising perspectives. Stand on Waterloo Bridge over the Thames, and you will feel an instant impact of the juxtaposition of new and old.

On the South Bank, it is the shock of the new that awaits the scanning eye. Once bordered by the corrugated-iron warehouses of Victorian overseas trade, the river now sports a new look, with interestingly shaped but unfinished-looking concrete palaces of art and culture. On the downriver side of the bridge is the National Theatre and on the upriver side, the Festival Hall complex of three concert halls, and the Arts Council's Hayward Gallery. In front of them, broad walks with gardens and young trees that will one day soften the severe outlines of the buildings behind give Londoners a pleasant place to stroll.

From the bridge, the seats of the government, law and commerce of Britain are seen in one great sweep along the north bank. To the west rise the Victorian gothic spires and towers of the Houses of Parliament, dominated by the clock

London's National Theatre is housed in one of a set of cultural buildings on the South Bank of the Thames. The modern complex provides a stimulating contrast to the older masterpieces of architecture such as St. Paul's across the river.

tower of Big Ben and the Victoria Tower of the House of Lords. To their right, east of Westminster Bridge, stands the solid bulk of government buildings which line Whitehall. Past Hungerford footbridge and the railway bridge from Charing Cross station are the Middle Temple and Inner Temple, two of the four Inns of Court, a fine area of buildings, many of which date back to the eighteenth century and whose medieval origins may still be traced in the layout of their lanes and alleyways. With their courts and lawns, they offer one of the pleasantest places for a stroll in all London.

Farther downriver, the great dome of St. Paul's Cathedral looks dwarfed by the towers of the banks and insurance companies that rise behind it in the City – dwarfed but not diminished, for Christopher Wren's masterpiece has an elegance and style that today's architects have yet to achieve.

Not many would dispute that this view from Waterloo Bridge is one of the noblest to be seen in any capital city. The rebirth of the river as a highway, as it was in Elizabethan times, means that there are many ways to enjoy it, both from the land and from the water. The riverside facade, though glorious, conceals the variety of London's many quarters, which can only be truly appreciated on foot, when the explorer can wander in and out of small side streets, steal a moment's peace in the City churches, trudge with the crowds along the busy shopping streets, or relax in the many parks.

In the City, the small but precisely defined and immensely rich part of London which, for most people, begins where the Strand is divided from Fleet Street by Temple Bar, the foundations go back to Roman times. Though plague, fire and war have ensured that there is little left in the way of buildings of the old City, its original shape and lay-outs still dictate its modern plan. London Wall, running today from Aldersgate almost to Bishopsgate, was the location of part of the wall the Romans built, and the City centre at the Bank of England has the familiar look of a Roman Forum, with its temples represented by the Victorian-style Royal Exchange and the Mansion House, and its basilica by today's bank buildings. Tradition is strong in the City; its very institutions, which include such establishments as the City Livery Companies, are the descendants of the various guilds of medieval trades, and its street names – Old Jewry, Ironmonger Lane, Candlewick Street, for example – remain to remind the passer-by of their former residents. The City that exists today grew up after the 1666 Fire of London, which is commemorated by the Monument, a 202-foot (62-m) column near Pudding Lane, where the Fire started, and from the top of which there are fine views. Christopher Wren played a major part in the rebuilding of the City, and his churches are still a fine presence, despite the devastation of World War II; later, Victorian and Edwardian princes of commerce added their share of buildings.

On the whole, the City is a male domain, dominated by those on whom the responsibility for conducting the serious business of finance rests. The West End of London, which is devoted very much to the luxury trades and entertainment, is, by contrast, much more a woman's world – a broad generalization, true, but there is an undeniable charm and femininity about the West End, evident as much in its architecture as in the activities and pastimes it promotes.

Piccadilly Circus, Leicester Square, and Trafalgar Square, presided over by Landseer's lions and the facade of the National Gallery, have been the West End's traditional gathering places for decades, where all kinds and conditions of people may be encountered day and night. The recent renaissance of the old

The powerful figure of Winston Churchill by Ivor Roberts Jones stands in Parliament Square with statues of other great statesmen like Lincoln, Smuts and Disraeli. The clock tower of the New Palace of Westminster was built by Sir Charles Barry in 1840–50 and houses the great bell known as Big Ben.

Left: This statue of a merman and dolphins enlivens one of the Trafalgar Square fountains. In the background is the National Gallery, built in 1838 by William Wilkins to house the pictures owned by John Angerstein, which formed the basis of one of the finest collections of paintings in the world.

Covent Garden fruit and vegetable market (now moved south of the Thames to Nine Elms) into a smart precinct of shops and cafés has given central London a new social focal point.

Lively, if not always elegant, Piccadilly Circus, Leicester Square and the maze of streets between the two in the Soho area are where the neon lights flash, the enticements are often shamelessly displayed and a sort of medieval atmosphere is presided over by street entertainers, con men, tourists, fruit-stall owners and those who work in the neighbourhood mingling night and day. This is also the heart of London's commercial theatreland, and the theatre signs glitter in avenues and streets between the Circus and the Strand.

A few steps off Piccadilly, the broad street that leads into the Circus, lies another world of smart shops in the elegant arcades that run off the main street and the quietly expensive flats and restaurants of Mayfair. Beyond, there is Bond Street and then a world of great hotels, sophisticated and exclusive restaurants and clubs, and the vast area of parkland – Green Park, St. James's Park, Hyde Park, and Kensington Gardens – where the palaces – Buckingham, St. James's and Kensington – may be found.

Walk south from Hyde Park and you come to Knightsbridge, an area of internationally famous department stores and of exclusive boutiques, many of them along Beauchamp Place, and Sloane Street, which leads into Sloane Square and from which issues the Kings Road, where the spirit of once-swinging London of the sixties still breathes, albeit more quietly.

The Royal Borough of Kensington and Chelsea, in which these areas of London are situated, has long-established claims to being a breeding ground of culture. Sir Thomas More lived here and so did Thomas Carlyle, Oscar Wilde and Henry James; among the many painters to have had studios here were J. M. W. Turner, James McNeill Whistler and that elegant painter of the English scene and the English horse, Sir Alfred Munnings. The borough also has one of the largest complexes of museums in the world, including the Victoria and Albert Museum, the Science Museum and Natural History Museum, the latter a remarkable example in architecture of the Victorian genius for plagiarism.

Things have changed, of course, since the characters of the various quarters of London first began to find their distinctive shapes; frontiers have been smudged and definitions amended, with the changes being traced, perhaps accidentally, by those mirrors of national and metropolitan life we call the media. Appropriately

The Barbican Centre, London's new art and leisure centre built near the fort on the old Roman wall, has two theatres, a concert hall, three cinemas, art galleries and restaurants. There is an exotic sub-tropical garden in a vast rooftop greenhouse.

The famous Covent Garden fruit and vegetable market, named after the convent garden which existed here from the thirteenth century, has moved to the south bank of the Thames. In its place Londoners have gained a new leisure area, where boutiques, market stalls, restaurants and snack bars attract hundreds of visitors daily. Among the many attractions are the street buskers who entertain the crowds with dance, music, mime or demonstrations of magic.

enough, the media are traditionally centred near the bastions of the law in Fleet Street and between the City and Westminster upriver, though pressures of space have obliged radio and television stations to set up their empires outside this area.

Apart from St. Bride's Church, Fleet Street on the whole can show no significant buildings, though there are some notable period pieces such as the black-glass-fronted Daily Express headquarters. This, no doubt, is appropriate for such ephemeral business as the purveying of news. But in the newspapers, much more than on radio or television, is reflected the whole of London. The discussions in Parliament, the ceremonies at Westminster Abbey, the royal events at Buckingham Palace, the trials at the Old Bailey, and the behaviour of the Stock Exchange are meat and drink for Fleet Street, but so too are happenings of interest only to Londoners themselves.

In the nineteenth century, London's newspapers would also have reported on the goings-on in London's ports, that great area beyond London Bridge and the

Above right: The amazing Romanesque-style building in Cromwell Road, South Kensington, the museum centre of London, was created by Alfred Waterhouse in 1873–80. It houses the five departments of the Natural History Museum, which originated in the collections of Sir Hans Sloane.

Tower of London where riverside docks were once packed with ships that carried passengers and goods to and from the farthest parts of the British Empire. Despite the closure of the old docks in recent years, dockland and the East End are still colourful areas with small businesses and factories and a Jewish quarter on the fringe of the City, where shops, stores and markets such as Petticoat Lane and Bermondsey are open on a Sunday and provide the most lively shopping scenes in London.

South and north of the River Thames, the land rises gently to higher ground: in the south to the London residential areas built up during the turn of the century round the open spaces of Clapham and Wandsworth Commons, full of streets of solid Edwardian terraces and red-brick mansions; in the north to the heights of Hampstead and Highgate, which were popular residential areas even in early Georgian times. On the way to these fine viewpoints of London Town, one passes the long east-to-west shopping area of Oxford Street and, farther north and running parallel to it, the Marylebone Road. It was this part of London that history chose as the birthplace of its rail network, for here, just north of present-day Euston Station, the engineer Richard Trevithick demonstrated his engine on rails in 1809 and thereby set Britain on a course of railway development which opened up transport throughout the world. On or near Marylebone Road lie several of London's great railway termini: Paddington, Euston, King's Cross and that neo-Gothic masterpiece, St. Pancras. These are the gateways to the north and west, just as Waterloo and Victoria Stations are the departure points to the south and south-east.

Past the canals of north London, which once carried barges laden with goods from dockland to all parts of Britain, the land rises more steeply to the ridge of hills to which Londoners fled during the plague years. Hampstead's Vale of Health was so named because it was a refuge during these years. From the top of the Heath, once a haunt of highwaymen, there is a wonderful view of London which Constable painted and which Keats, who lived in Hampstead, must have loved to gaze upon. From the heights one looks over the wooded Heath, with its copses and lakes; one of these is the source of the old River Fleet, which now flows underground but gave its name to the street. The whole city is laid

*The once busy docks of the Port of London are now being converted to leisure use. St. Katharine's Dock, by Tower Bridge, is surrounded by refurbished warehouses, and in its waters floats a splendid collection of old craft, including the **Discovery**, Scott's polar ship.*

out below, from the East End to the West End, with the hills of the Dulwich and Crystal Palace areas rising on the southern horizon. It is a breathtaking sight on a clear day and, seen from the rural surroundings of the Heath, a summing-up not only of London but of the whole of Britain in its mixture of nineteenth-century industrial and commercial development and rural charm.

Around London

When first established, the tiny villages that were to become today's cities tended to huddle for protection within a wall, or to cling to the protective might of castles. Later, when the power of the city grew and the enemy without was subdued or incorporated into the system, the life of the city moved outwards and the rich and powerful began to think of palaces and mansions set in parks and gardens outside the overcrowded confines of the walled town. This process has left some of the richest treasures of London, and some of the most beautiful and historically interesting houses in Britain, on its outskirts.

Downriver from the Tower of London lies Greenwich, best reached by a boat trip through the fascinating expanse of docks built during the enormously successful overseas trading years of the nineteenth century. With its hillside park, on whose crest sits the old Royal Observatory where Greenwich Mean Time was first measured. The village grew during the Tudor period, when British sailors roamed the seven seas and brought back fabulously rich troves, not only of gold and silver, but also of spices, silks, and such extraordinary new additions to the kitchen as potatoes, tomatoes, and maize, as well as tobacco. The old palace, a favourite residence of Henry VII and Henry VIII no longer exists. In its place is the splendid sequence of buildings by Wren, Hawksmoor and Vanbrugh, begun as a naval hospital in the reign of William and Mary, but now used as the home of the Royal Naval College. Among the buildings, the Chapel and the superb Banqueting Hall can be visited.

Behind the Royal Naval College and across the Romsey Road lies the elegant building of the Queen's House, designed by Inigo Jones for James I's wife, Anne of Denmark, and finished in the time of Henrietta Maria, wife of Charles I. The National Maritime Museum is housed in the Queen's House and adjacent buildings, which are connected by a splendid colonnade. The whole magnificent complex of buildings and its lovely setting, seen from the river or from the hill behind, has few equals anywhere in the world.

Towering above a dry dock by the river's edge, the masts of the *Cutty Sark* reveal the presence of the last of the tea clippers and, next to it, is tiny *Gipsy*

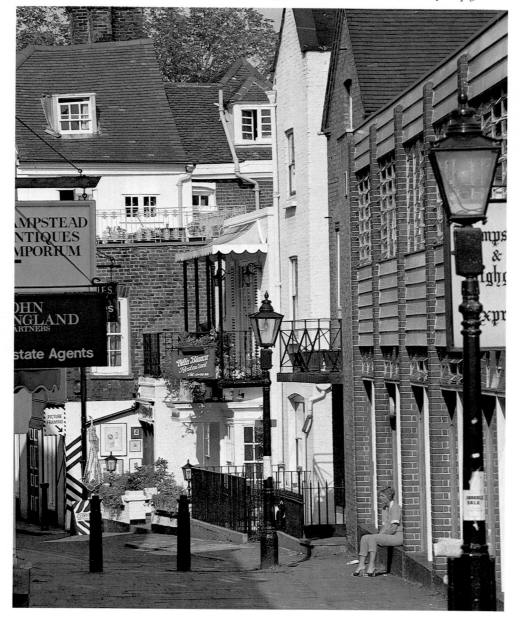

Perrins Court, in Hampstead, typifies the studied picturesqueness of many of the streets and lanes of this North London suburb. Though surrounded by Victorian and Edwardian red-brick mansions, Hampstead village itself manages to maintain an old-world rural atmosphere, thanks in part to its proximity to the Heath.

Overleaf: The fine buildings of the Royal Naval College (formerly Greenwich Hospital) by Sir Christopher Wren occupy the site of Henry VII's palace of Placentia, where both Elizabeth I and her sister Mary were born. Today, the buildings flank the avenue leading to the Queen's House, the first Palladian-style building in Britain, built by Inigo Jones for Anne of Denmark but lived in by Henrietta Maria, wife of Charles I.

The increased probability of the Thames overflowing its banks has led to the construction of a barrier at Silvertown in the Woolwich Reach. Seen here in the distance, the barrier crosses a stretch of river once crowded with liners and cargo ships.

Moth IV, in which Sir Francis Chichester circumnavigated the globe single-handed. The town of Greenwich lies mostly to the west of the Naval College. Blackheath, a pleasant open common adjoining Greenwich, is also a sought-after residential area.

Across the River Thames to the north stretches the Lea Valley, today surrounded by housing but in Tudor times a great expanse of open country, of which there remains only the 6,000 acres (2,428 hectares) of Epping Forest. In the Lea Valley to the west of the Forest lies Waltham Abbey, an early Norman church which is the burial place of King Harold, who was killed at the battle of Hastings. To the south of the forest a well-preserved, half-timbered house which was once Queen Elizabeth I's hunting lodge reminds us that Epping is the remains of a once royal hunting forest.

The River Lea rises in the Chiltern Hills, a range of low chalk hills which slope gently south to the London Basin, with here and there an escarpment to add drama to what was once countryside but is now suburbia. These hills marked a frontier between London and points north; battles, such as Barnet during the Civil War, were fought here, and stage coaches, after their long climb out of London, had a change of horses at the staging inns along the crests of the hills. From here the northern slopes slid down to the upper valleys of the Lea and the Ver, which runs through St. Albans.

The stretch of countryside between the two rivers was popular even in the times of the ancient Britons, but it was the Romans who built the great city of Verulamium, whose ruins can be seen in the park though which the river flows. On the hill above the Roman town the Normans built another and topped it with one of England's great abbeys. This magnificent building, which includes a Roman brick tower, was dedicated to St. Alban, a Christian Roman who was martyred here.

A few miles to the north of St. Albans is Ayot St. Lawrence, a pilgrimage spot for admirers of the satirical playwright George Bernard Shaw, and to the south is one of the greatest of Jacobean houses, Hatfield House. The Old Palace of Hatfield, which was the home of Elizabeth I as a young girl and in whose

gardens she heard the news of her sister Mary's death and her accession, has partly survived and stands alongside the superb mansion built by Robert Cecil, Earl of Salisbury, Elizabeth's Secretary of State and ancestor of the present Marquess of Salisbury, whose home this is. This splendid house, with its vast wood-panelled rooms, contains mementoes of Elizabeth and a portrait of her by the great English miniaturist Nicholas Hilliard. Visitors may lunch or take tea in the Old Palace, where Elizabeth held her first Privy Council.

Due west of Hatfield towards Hertford lies another great mansion built in Tudor Times but rebuilt in the nineteenth-century Gothic style. This is Knebworth House, home of the Lytton family, which includes Lord Lytton, the novelist, among its descendants. The house contains eighteenth-century memorabilia and relics of Imperial India. To the east of Hertford, itself a town that retains a great deal of the atmosphere of pre-industrial Britain, is the interesting village of Much Hadham, a remarkably unspoiled village. Once the seat of the Bishops of London, it still contains their Jacobean palace, a twelfth-century church and many other fine old buildings.

West of St. Albans, the Chiltern Hills curve south-west towards the River Thames enclosing other favourite royal areas on the outskirts of London. First comes Richmond-upon-Thames, partly set on a hill above the Thames and Kew. Henry VII had a palace at Richmond, and some fragments of it can still be seen by elegant Richmond Green, which in Henry VII's time was the scene of the festivals and tournaments that the king enjoyed. Mary Tudor also lived here while she was married to Philip II of Spain, and Queen Elizabeth I died here in 1603. The grounds of the palace stretched down to the river and into what is now the Old Deer Park, the western border of the Royal Botanic Garden, Kew, a world centre of botanical research and one of the most beautiful of London's parks. In Kew Gardens is the red-brick Dutch House, also known as Kew Palace, lived in by George III, whose mother, Augusta, Princess of Wales, was instrumental in establishing the great garden there.

Kew and Richmond form one of the loveliest and most stylish parts of outer London. In addition to their situation on the Thames, which, flowing east from

Epping Forest is all that remains of the royal forest of Waltham and, despite its urban surroundings, it still has plenty of wild deer, foxes, squirrels and weasels. The forest is bounded by the River Lea to the west and the Roding to the east.

Left: Richmond-upon-Thames was a favourite home of the Tudor kings, who were evidently not worried by the danger of flooding as their palace was built by the river. Most of the houses of Richmond were built on the hill which rises above the frequently flooded east bank.

the lovely heartland of England, becomes tidal below Teddington Lock near Richmond, these outer suburbs of London are also connected to the Midlands via the Grand Union Canal, which enters the Thames at Brentford, opposite Kew.

Also across the River from Kew Gardens is Syon House, which belongs to the Duke of Northumberland and has one of the finest Robert Adam interiors in Britain, as well as a superb garden and garden centre.

Upriver to the south of Richmond is Ham House, an early seventeenth-century mansion later refurbished by the Duke of Lauderdale, a friend of Charles II. The villages of Ham and Petersham, nearby, have several houses of the same period which preserve the atmosphere of the past, among them Douglas House, Montrose House, Petersham House and Manor House. The best view of the River Thames at this point is from the hill terrace above Richmond where Joshua Reynolds had his house. Here he painted the scene which also inspired innumerable other painters, including Turner.

From the terrace it is just a short walk to Richmond Park, which stretches south to Wimbledon Common and eastwards as far as Putney. This bit of rural England in suburban London has lakes, duck-ponds, trees, herds of deer, and several splendid houses, one of which houses the Royal Ballet School. From the park's high ground there are lovely views across Petersham and Ham and the River Thames and northwards, on a clear day, as far as the high ground of Hampstead and Highgate.

The concentration of royal and noble houses to the west side of London as far as Windsor led to the creation of great residential districts for those connected with the court either as courtiers or servants. Twickenham, stretching between Richmond and Bushy Park, was one such. At the northern end of Twickenham, near the Thames, is York House, named after James II and lived in by Charles II's Lord Chancellor, Edward Hyde, whose daughter married James and gave birth to the future queens, Mary and Anne. Nearby, to the south, is Marble Hill, a fine Palladian-style villa built in the 1720s by Henrietta Howard, a mistress of George II, and later lived in by Mrs. Fitzherbert, morganatic wife of George, Prince of Wales, who became Prince Regent and George IV. Yet another very remarkable house in Twickenham is Strawberry Hill, created in the Gothic style

Below: The view from Richmond Hill looking down towards Ham was much admired by smart London society of the eighteenth century, who built their houses here and at Marble Hill across the river. By the river's edge in the town of Richmond are the remains of the Tudor palace in which Elizabeth I died, and above the hill is Richmond Park.

by Horace Walpole, the eighteenth-century wit and writer of Gothic novels.

To the north of Twickenham and west of Isleworth, with its pleasant little riverside frontage which includes the old London Apprentice pub, lies an industrial area crossed by the two great roads out of London to the west, the M4 motorway and the A4 (the Great West Road). Sandwiched between the two is another once-great Tudor estate, Osterley, built by Sir Thomas Gresham, founder of the Royal Exchange. During the eighteenth century the house was almost entirely rebuilt by Robert Adam, who left in it some of his finest work. The Osterley estate is still large, but cut by the motorway.

A drive back towards central London on the A4 from Osterley leads to Chiswick House, now hemmed in by London's residential sprawl. Once in the grounds suburbia is soon forgotten, however, as the mansion, surrounded by trees and set by an ornamental lake, creates a world of its own from which the

Osterley Park was built by the famous Tudor banker Sir Thomas Gresham and remodelled by a subsequent owner, Sir William Chambers. It was finished by Robert Adam, who designed the imposing portico and much of the interior. The park round the house is extensive and includes three lakes.

sound of the traffic rushing by outside fades away into a hum. Chiswick House was built by the Earl of Burlington, who recreated this model Italian mansion in the Palladian style with the help of Italian architects. Socially, the house reached its apogee in the early nineteenth century when it was in the hands of the Duchess of Devonshire, whose salons included the more radical politicians of the time, such as George Canning and Charles James Fox.

Alongside Chiswick House stands a more humble building, the home of the painter William Hogarth. His genius was, in part at least, dedicated to satirizing the antics of his splendid neighbours, and his work now hangs in Chiswick House as well as in his own Hogarth House which is a museum of his work. In Hogarth's time the land around him and to the west was farmland but nothing of this remains today. Instead the traffic roars past on its way to and from Heathrow airport and beyond.

Still to the west of London, and upriver from Richmond is a stretch of truly royal river. At Hampton Court the Thames, which has been wending its way eastwards from Windsor, Egham and Chertsey, suddenly curves sharply north around a fertile wooded area. Here Cardinal Wolsey, Chancellor of England, chose, when at the height of his power, a site for a palace to outrival that of the king, Henry VIII. Such presumption brought him no good but left to posterity one of England's most beautiful palaces. Wolsey's palace was added to by Henry, after he had wrested it from the disgraced cardinal, and later by William III, who had the good sense to employ Christopher Wren to take charge of the work. The result of the various additions is a glorious complex of buildings that have the living quality of architecture brought about by slow growth in the hands of a variety of talented people.

Romantically, Hampton Court Palace has no equal, for it is associated with Catherine of Aragon, Anne Boleyn, Jane Seymour and Catherine Howard, whose unfortunate ghost is supposed to wander in the Haunted Gallery. Its gardens are also unrivalled by those of any other royal palace. These show the influence of Dutch King William and his wife Mary, whose enthusiasm for the Dutch style gave a more lively aspect to the grounds, which had previously been laid out in a more formal French fashion. The Maze, which is one of the attractions for visitors, also dates from this period. Adjoining Hampton Court to the north is Bushy Park, where deer wander among the chestnut trees. The park was conceived by Wren as the route to the north front of the palace.

Perhaps the most famous of all the royal residences to the west of London is Windsor Castle. Although some distance upriver from Hampton Court, modern transport has brought Windsor so close to London that it seems appropriate to describe it here. Still lived in by the Royal Family, Windsor Castle has a history that dates back to Edward the Confessor, though it was William the Conqueror who built the first wooden hunting lodge here. The stone castle began to rise in the reign of Henry II, who also started the formidable Round Tower which separates the upper and lower wards of the castle. Like the State Apartments, the Round Tower cannot be visited today when the Queen is in residence.

Right: The sophisticated 3rd Earl of Burlington, patron of the arts, built Chiswick House in the style of a Palladian villa. Edward VII was a frequent visitor to the villa during his youth. The park, designed by William Kent and carried out in a delightful Italian style, has an ornamental lake.

Below: The River Thames in London has inspired many painters including Whistler and Monet, whose misty riverscapes are recalled by the view from Hammersmith.

Around the vast castle which dominates Windsor are enchanting little streets which descend to the Thames and are also found across the river at Eton. By the castle entrance is Church Street, close to the High Street and the Parish Church.

Preceding pages: Cardinal Wolsey's famous palace by the Thames, at Hampton Court, is a magnificent structure which he unwillingly gave to Henry VIII in a vain attempt to keep his favour. The east and south wings were added later by Sir Christopher Wren at the command of William III.

One of the glories of Windsor Castle is St. George's Chapel, the chapel of the Order of the Garter, whose knights' stalls and banners line the interior. Begun during the reign of Edward IV, and completed in the sixteenth century, it is one of the finest examples of Perpendicular Gothic architecture in England, comparable in beauty to King's College Chapel in Cambridge. Several kings are buried within its walls, including Henry VIII, Edward IV and Charles I. The Albert Memorial Chapel alongside was built for Henry VI, though it was Cardinal Wolsey who completed it. Queen Victoria decided to make it into a memorial to Albert, though the prince consort's body lies at Frogmore to the east of the castle in Home Park. The mausoleum also contains the remains of Edward VIII, the Duke of Windsor.

Eton College lies on the edge of Windsor, across Windsor Bridge (a footbridge). Founded in the fifteenth century, the college and its superb chapel are the main objects of interest in Eton village. Stretching south from Windsor Castle and town is the vast Great Park, one of the most popular attractions of Windsor. In its 2,000 acres (over 800 hectares) are polo fields, at Smith's Lawn, and a safari park, and many events take place in the park during summer.

Around Windsor much of the country remains rural, although new residential estates continue to erode it. To the south and west, farming country still predominates, as it does to the north beyond the industrial belt of Slough, where many villages, often dormitories for London commuters, have retained their rural character. Among these are Gerrards Cross and Beaconsfield, to the south of which lie the lovely woods of Burnham Beeches, a reminder of the beauty that once surrounded the capital of Britain before the industrial age.

The Eastern Counties

The east coast of England between the Humber and the Thames includes the counties of Lincoln, Norfolk, Suffolk and Essex. Here among the flat or undulating farmlands lie some of England's oldest roots, laid down by invaders who came across the sea and settled. The Romans came from Gaul, founding cities at Colchester, Caister, Brancaster and Caistor St. Edmund to the south of Norwich. When their departure left a power gap, the Angles and Saxons moved in, followed by the Vikings and, finally, by William the Conqueror, thrusting up from his southern base. He was resisted by Hereward the Wake in the remote fenlands, just as the Romans had been by Boadicea, who was also leader of an eastern England tribe, the Iceni.

Later, there would be more peaceful invaders; the Dutch arrived to teach the East Anglians how to drain their marshes and turn them into rich agricultural land, and Flemish weavers came to carry on their trade on the slopes of the wolds, where sheep provided their raw materials. Trade with the continent of Europe involved the Hanseatic traders, a commerce continued today with Germany, the Netherlands and Denmark.

Stratford St. Mary is a small village on the River Stour in the Suffolk countryside that was John Constable's home and inspiration. There are many fine timbered buildings in the village and one of them is the Priest's House.

During the Tudor period the eastern counties, rich in farming lands, were centres of power. Thomas Howard, Earl of Norfolk, who occupied the great Norman fortification of Castle Rising, near King's Lynn, was responsible for the fall of Cardinal Wolsey, himself an East Anglian. Mary Tudor also lived in Castle Rising, whose ruins may still be seen two miles (3 km) or so north of King's Lynn. Among other historical personages who came from the eastern counties were Oliver Cromwell, born in Huntingdon, and Horatio Nelson, born at Burnham Thorpe.

Since the Industrial Revolution, with its emphasis on coal, iron and manufacturing, rural and agricultural East Anglia seems to have faded from the centre of the national stage. Perhaps this has been all to the good for, although commerce flourishes in East Anglian ports and the farmlands are much more productive than in the eighteenth century, when Thomas Coke revolutionized English farming from his home at Holkham Hall near the north Norfolk coast, the eastern counties have managed to remain remarkably unspoiled. No motorways carve their way across the tranquil landscape, and no vast industrial conurbation spreads across its green checkerboard. Except for large resorts like Great Yarmouth and Clacton, or areas like the Norfolk Broads, even the tourist business has failed to creat those agglomerations which make travel a penance as well as a hazard. This is all to the benefit of those who enjoy a natural countryside where the social communities are small and where traditional trades and crafts still survive.

From the Humber to the Thames

In Lincolnshire, the northernmost county of eastern England, a ridge of limestone hills runs from north to south, a natural defence except where the River Withan breaches the hills. This is guarded by Lincoln, a city where evidence of Roman occupation can still be seen and dominated by an imposing twelfth- to fourteenth-century cathedral rising 365 feet (111 m) above the hilltop and surrounded by the picturesque old town. Between Lincoln and the coast of the Wash stretches fertile flat land where bulb fields are a blaze of colour in spring. Not surprisingly, this area is known as Holland and Dutch-style houses are not uncommon.

Although there are big ports like Harwich, Lowestoft, Great Yarmouth, King's Lynn and Grimsby, and big holiday resorts like Skegness, Clacton and Southend around the coasts of the eastern counties, the general impression is one of a sparsely inhabited shore, with small villages whose harbours are crammed as much with every kind of leisure craft as with fishing and other commercial craft.

Along the Norfolk coast the land seems little higher than the sea, except at Hunstanton, where low cliffs edge the grassy slopes of the resort. Curiously, this resort faces west, for it lies on the curving coastline around the southern edge of the Wash, an extensive tidal bay in which King John managed to lose the Crown Jewels. At the eastern corner of the bay lies King's Lynn, on the River Ouse. Once one of England's most important ports, King's Lynn is now an attractive market town, preserving many interesting buildings from its great days, including the seventeenth-century Greenland Fishery building and a handsome Customs House, built in 1683 and wonderfully well preserved. The main shopping centre has, alas, been a victim of the developers and is now a characterless shopping precinct. Near King's Lynn is Sandringham House, country home of the Royal Family, where the gardens and an exhibition of royal motor cars can be seen when the Royal Family is not in residence.

Towards the east the Norfolk coast curves gently southwards and is bordered by saltings – low-lying, grass-covered marshlands – sometimes covered by high tides. Created by the silting of the shoreline, the saltings now separate the fishing villages from the sea, and communication is maintained by canals meandering through them. Instead of diminishing the sea-going atmosphere, the saltings seem to increase it. Boats of every kind line the canal banks and crowd into the tiny harbours of the coastal villages, where fishermen live alongside holiday boat people in the flint cottages which edge the narrow streets. A reminder that these villages once, but no longer, were by the sea lies in their names. Cley next the Sea and Wells-next-the-Sea are particularly attractive, the former's saltings being one of the most renowned bird sanctuaries in Britain and the latter having a reputation for providing most of the whelks sold in Britain.

More conventional, though still small, resorts along this Norfolk coast are Cromer and Sheringham, both with sandy beaches along the edge of the town and with all the usual holiday amenities, though not on the scale of Great Yarmouth, the vast Norfolk holiday playground farther south along the sandy coast.

Great Yarmouth lives a double life. Along the Marine Parade, which edges the extensive sandy beach, there is all the garish fairground exuberance characteristic of large English seaside resorts. An amusement park with big dippers, a ferris wheel, dodgems, spiders, whips and all the other hair-raising machinery usual to such places, two piers, gardens, theatres, snack bars, souvenir shops, fortune-tellers, weight-guessers, and other entertainers provide a panoramic view of the British at play. Barely half a mile (800 m) away and running parallel with the front for two miles (3 km) is the harbour, built along the banks of the River Yare, which runs into the sea through Breydon Water. Here, Great Yarmouth reveals itself to be a busy seaport, with freighters that ply between Britain and the Continent and ships that supply the oil rigs out in the North Sea. From these quaysides there is a constant coming and going of pleasure craft bound for sea trips or for cruises into the waterways of the Broads that lie inland.

Lowestoft, farther to the south in Suffolk, is another port with a double identity. Though no longer the centre of the herring fishing industry as it once was, the town still has a large trawler fleet and large docks for North Sea ships. The resort lies to the south of the harbour, and like Great Yarmouth, has two piers and all the fun of the fair.

Between Lowestoft and Felixstowe, the Essex resort to the south, the coast seems almost deserted, as if the encroaching sea has won the battle for possession, as indeed it did at Dunwich, where all that remains of the thriving medieval town is part of the graveyard and a few cottages; the rest is under the sea, including the church, whose tower finally vanished in 1919. People say that on quiet evenings the ghostly sound of its bells may be heard beneath the waters. There are two exceptionally attractive villages on this coast, however. One of these, Aldeburgh, is world-famous as a musical centre, a fame begun by Benjamin

The Shire Hall in the handsome town of Woodbridge, on the River Deben in Suffolk, was built in the sixteenth century by Thomas Seckford. Across the river is Sutton Hoo, where a Saxon ship and treasure were discovered in 1939.

Britten, who lived here, and its June Festival, held in the town and in the Maltings at nearby Snape, fills it with musicians and music lovers from all over the world. The other, Southwold, has been saved from commercial development by its isolated, marsh-surrounded situation, and it retains an eighteenth-century atmosphere carefully preserved by its residents, whose pride in their village can be seen on every painted house front and in every flowering window-box.

As the coast winds on southwards its character changes. Long estuaries, providing perfect havens for yachts and cruisers, stretch inland to Woodbridge, near which, at Sutton Hoo, a great Saxon treasure was discovered, to Ipswich and to Colchester. The estuaries, bordered by low-lying grasslands, are good bird-watching territory, and many varieties of geese, herons, swans, and other wildfowl are plentiful.

Although within easy reach of London, the coast is still sparsely inhabited here, and many parts of it can only be reached on foot along the coastal paths.

The character of the towns and resorts vary considerably and range from busy ports like Harwich, popular resorts like Clacton and Southend, and sedate seaside residential towns like Frinton, to villages of weatherboard houses like Brightlingsea and Burnham-on-Crouch, where the masts of the sailing fraternity's boats are as thick as trees in Epping Forest.

Exploring the coast of the eastern counties by car is an easy business, though not one for those in a hurry. The roads wind gently through the countryside, and in the indented southern coastline of Essex and Suffolk long detours are often necessary to reach villages and towns by the sea. In the north, the road runs close to the coast but seldom close enough or high enough to provide sea views. As if in compensation, a detour of a mile or less will usually bring the traveller quickly to villages with a special character not found outside the eastern counties.

Norwich and the Broads

No one knows exactly how this vast area of shallow lakes, joined by rivers and canals, in eastern Norfolk was formed; some attribute it to glacial erosion, while others believe the land was excavated by people digging for peat. Whatever the cause, the result is a safe, unspoiled watery kingdom where thousands of people each summer sail their craft over more than 200 miles (322 km) of rivers and lakes edged by woods and fields. The main Broads – Wroxham, Barton, Hickling, Ormesby and Filby – are linked by the River Bure and its tributaries, while the River Yare makes the cathedral city of Norwich accessible by water from the coast.

Right: Jacobean Blickling Hall in Norfolk was built in the seventeenth century on the site of an earlier house where, it is said, Anne Boleyn was born. The Hall, which was designed by Robert Lyminge, has a fine staircase, state rooms and portrait gallery and is surrounded by a 4,500-acre (1 821-hectare) park.

Although the Broads are best appreciated by those travelling on the water, there are also many roads by which a motorist can visit some of the enchanting villages that are the ports of call for waterborne visitors. At Horning, the whole village is a maze of canals bordered by the gardens of the inhabitants. Between Ormsby and Rollesby the road travels between the two great Broads. The latter village has a Norman church, and archaeologists have discovered that people lived around here 4,000 years ago. At Reedham, on the Yare, motorists have the unusual experience of crossing the river by a chain ferry and also of visiting a working taxidermist preparing stuffed animals and birds for museums and collectors.

Norwich lies at the western end of the Broads and the cathedral's 315-foot (96-m) spire can be seen from miles away. The tower and nave of the cathedral are Norman and other parts of it were added during the following centuries, but the whole is remarkably unified and, with its surrounding houses and lawns, is among the finest ecclesiastical complexes in Britain. Look out for the stone figure near St. Luke's Chapel, which dates from 1100 and may be Herbert de Losinga, the founder of the church.

The Norfolk Broads are a vast area of lakes and rivers usually crowded with yachts and cruisers in summer. At Horning Ferry on the River Bure the canals lap the lawns of the attractive village houses.

Right: Norwich Cathedral's imposing Norman tower, topped by a fifteenth-century spire, was often painted by Constable and other artists of the Norwich School. The open space of the cathedral close stretches past the Bishop's Palace to the River Wensum. To the south rises the keep of the Norman castle.

The castle, which is reached from the cathedral via the fourteenth-century Ethelbert Gate, was built in the twelfth century. In its imposing keep are several collections of porcelain, armour and – most interesting of all – paintings of the Norwich School. Below the castle is the open-air marketplace, usually a scene of lively activity every day. The market square is flanked by the City Hall to the west, the fifteenth-century Guildhall to the north and the church of St. Peter Mancroft to the south. Norwich is more than a collection of old buildings, however; it is the centre of Norfolk life and it preserves the true character of an English cathedral city.

Cambridge and the Fens

Like the Broads, the Fens are a low-lying area of land, but they lie to the north of the eastern counties, extending from the Wash in a sweep of green fields and marshland intersected by canals and rivers to the cities of Peterborough, Huntingdon, Cambridge and Ely, which stand like sentinels around the empty marshland area. Peterborough Cathedral strengthens this image and, with its solid and beautiful architecture, looks sometimes as much a stronghold against invaders as a building representing the spiritual life. Catherine of Aragon, Henry VIII's unhappy first wife, is buried here, and so was Mary Queen of Scots until her body was removed to Westminster Abbey.

Ely, another cathedral town on the southern borders of the Fens, was an island until the Fens were drained, and Hereward the Wake based his resistance to William the Conqueror on it. The present cathedral was begun by a supporter of William, and the original Norman architecture can be seen in the nave, transepts and west front. The remarkable octagonal tower, with its glorious Lantern, was

Left: The dykes which criss-cross the Fens around the Wash drain the water from the reclaimed land now devoted to farming and, in Lincolnshire, to large-scale daffodil and tulip culture. The work of reclaiming the land was inspired by the Dutch, who also influenced the local architecture.

built in the fourteenth century after the collapse of the original tower.

Huntingdon has no cathedral, and its renown rests on the plentiful evidence of the childhood of Oliver Cromwell. The house where he was born and the coaching inn belonging to his grandfather are still there. The grammar school which he attended is now a Cromwell museum, and his family home, Hinchingbroke House, a school. Around Huntingdon are some of the most charming of all Fenland villages; St. Ives, Hemingford Grey and Hemingford Abbots are all delightful places with old houses, some of them thatched, and all are well worth a visit.

Cambridge, though farther from the Fens than the other towns, nevertheless has a similar *raison d'être*. Originally a Roman outpost, it later became a Saxon stronghold, then a Norman military town guarding the people against the tribes that resisted Norman occupation. Its career as a centre of learning began much later, in the thirteenth century, when religious teachers set up courses of instruction for students who came eagerly from far and wide to acquire the new knowledge which was to transform the life of the nation. Out of this early enthusiasm grew the present university city, surely one of the most elegant in the world. The honey-coloured buildings stretching between the High Street and the River Cam provide visitors with walks through grassy squares surrounded by buildings dating back to Tudor times, past chapels and the halls where today's students, and – who knows? – tomorrow's leaders, reside. Some of the colleges stretch down to the Cam; others have lawns that border the water, where in summertime the students or visitors can glide slowly in punts along past the Backs, as the river-side is called. From the river there are few sights as memorable as the great square on which stands King's College Chapel, completed

Between Huntingdon and St. Ives the Great Ouse River flows through lovely countryside in which lie pretty old villages like Hemingford Abbots and Hemingford Grey. Houghton Mill, which dates back to the seventeenth century, is on the river near Wyton.

43

in 1515, one of the finest buildings in the Perpendicular style in the world.

Apart from the university the city of Cambridge has a busy commercial life, its industries including electronics and the manufacture of scientific instruments. A symbol of the old and new life of Cambridge is perhaps epitomized at Granchester, scene of the famous poem by Rupert Brooke, near which there stand today the giant saucers of the world's largest radio telescope.

Suffolk and Essex

The south-eastern part of the English eastern counties has an undulating terrain formed by the eastern extension of the Chiltern Hills.

Most of the Suffolk and Essex countryside is agricultural, dotted with many unspoiled little villages and watered by small streams that flow off the low hills towards the North Sea estuaries, where boats are as thick as sea birds. Church steeples, water towers and silos are the landmarks in this unruffled countryside, in which wide ditches drain fields where seas of corn and barley ripple in the summer breezes. It is also a part of England offering that quintessentially English sight: horses exercising over heathland, for Newmarket Heath, in the far west of Suffolk, has been the training ground of thoroughbred racehorses since Charles II's time.

After Edmund, the king of all East Anglia in the ninth century, was murdered by the Danes in 870, a shrine was set up for him in a monastery at what is today the town of Bury St. Edmunds, the county town of West Suffolk and centre point of the eastern counties. Not much remains of the original abbey, but there are two well-preserved gate-houses one of which is an impressive twelfth-century tower. One of the interesting features of the abbey church is the accretion of ruins of houses built in Tudor, Georgian and Victorian times. Readers of Dickens will remember that the Angel Hotel in Bury St. Edmunds was where Mr.

New Bridge, which crosses the River Cam behind St. John's College in Cambridge, was built in 1831 and nicknamed the Bridge of Sighs because of its resemblance to the famous Venetian bridge. The Cam flows through the Backs behind the colleges and past the glorious King's College Chapel.

Pickwick received the unwelcome news of a breach of promise action by Mrs. Bardell.

To the south-west of the town is the grand Ickworth House, set in a large park designed by Capability Brown, and furnished inside in eighteenth-century style, with a fine collection of Regency silver. It is a reminder that many noble houses were built in this part of Suffolk in past centuries.

From Bury St. Edmunds the land slopes away to the south and south-east, with farmlands and villages of great beauty scattered over the countryside. Many of these were medieval wool towns, which prospered when England's main trade to the Continent was in wool. Lavenham, to the south of Bury St. Edmunds, was one of these and its Wool Hall, incorporated in the Swan Hotel, bears out the importance of the town in those days. There are many half-timbered buildings dating from medieval times in this much visited showplace, and a church with an impressive tower built by one of the rich clothiers of the town.

Another interesting town with a fine main street full of attractive buildings is Long Melford, lying south of Bury St. Edmunds and a centre for the rich farmland around it. In this area there are many fine houses, such as Melford Hall and moated Kentwell Hall, both dating from Tudor times.

The River Stour that runs through Long Melford and then Sudbury, the birthplace of Thomas Gainsborough, whose father's Tudor house is now a museum, is the Stour that John Constable so often painted. As it approaches the sea it runs through Dedham Vale and the village of Dedham, whose church appears in several of Constable's paintings. East Bergholt, Constable's birthplace, is nearby and has changed little since his day; both his parents and his wife Maria are buried in the churchyard. Constable's home was at Flatford Mill, a place of pilgrimage for all who admire the great English painter's work. Willy Lott's cottage, the river and even the trees are still there, like models preserved in suspended time.

South of here lies the once great Roman city of Colchester, in whose massive castle keep, built over a temple ordered by the emperor Claudius, is a great collection of antiquities including Roman coins. One of the oldest cities in Britain and the town of Old King Cole, or King Cunobelin of the ancient Britons, Colchester is a thriving modern city that has retained many old quarters.

From Colchester, a road runs due west to an endearing corner of Essex. The low undulating land here is full of yet more enchanting eastern counties villages. Great Dunmow is famous for its legendary flitch of bacon which, according to tradition, is presented each year to the married couple who have not said a cross word to each other during the entire year.

The Rodings, eight villages, are scattered along the River Roding. Each of them has picturesque houses, half-timbered cottages, and wooded farmlands surrounding them. To the north of this unspoiled agricultural corner of Essex is Saffron Walden, also a town with fine medieval and Georgian houses, and an earthwork in which skeletons of Saxon inhabitants have been discovered.

To the west is one of the mansions of Thomas Howard, Earl of Suffolk. This is Audley End, whose present elegance is due to the work done by Robert Adam in the eighteenth century. The gardens of the house are also splendid and contain summerhouses, a temple and other architectural features.

Though only 40 miles (64 km) from London, this part of Essex has remained quite unspoiled by its proximity to the metropolis. Local residents desire to keep it this way and thus are understandably resisting plans to make Stansted, which lies between the Rodings and Saffron Walden, London's third airport.

Willy Lott's cottage is one of the most famous houses in Suffolk, thanks to Constable's famous painting. The cottage is at Flatford, where the Constable family mill has become a tourist shrine.

Southern England

Just 22 miles, or 35 kilometres, of sea separate the coast of the south of England – in which we include Hampshire, Sussex, Kent and parts of Wiltshire and Surrey – from the Continent of Europe at Dover. From here west to Beachy Head, where the South Downs take a dizzy dive into the sea, lie beaches invaded by foreign armies from Roman to Norman times. Julius Caesar came ashore near Deal in 55 BC, another Roman force landed farther east in AD 43, and William of Normandy came in pursuit of the English crown in 1066. After that, except for an impudent Dutch incursion up the Thames in the seventeenth century, England was never again invaded by foreign foes, though immigrants arrived, and still arrive, at these hospitable shores.

There are no great natural harbours along this Kent coast, which is either flat and marshy around the eastern tip or faced along the southern shore with the famous white cliffs which are both a frontier and a symbol of 'England, Home and Beauty'.

The coastline itself rises and falls in sweeps ranging from the sublime to the nondescript; behind is a beautiful countryside of hills and downs, rich farmlands, orchards and parklands, rivers and forests, which for centuries have made this one of the most desirable residential areas of Britain. Much of it retains the rural

The village of Headcorn lies amid the farmlands and woods that cover the undulating countryside of the Kentish Weald and has some fine timbered houses. One named 'Tilden', which has two neighbouring oast-houses where hops for beer making are dried, was built in 1430.

The River Medway, which once sheltered the Elizabethan fleets, has always been an important waterway through Kent. Thames sailing barges were the vessels used for transport along these inland waterways.

atmosphere of olden times, with small villages where thatched cottages crouch below the hedgerows or conical oast-houses rise above them, where old country pubs welcome more local folk than visitors, where amateurs play cricket at weekends on centuries-old village greens. This is the England poets have written about with dreamy metaphors and the languor of Keats' *Ode to a Nightingale*: this is the England of peace and country houses, and an orderly life, the England to which most Britons from industrial areas and cities escape for weekends or the summer holiday.

The two great sweeps of the North and South Downs, with the Weald of Kent between them, give variety to the landscape of the eastern part of this corner of England, while to the west the rich farms and woodlands of the Hampshire Basin glide gently down to Southampton and its sheltered waters.

The Coast

The coast of the southern counties detaches itself from the Thames estuary near Rochester, where a Norman keep and cathedral still stand, and Chatham, once a great naval shipyard established by Henry VIII but now under threat of closure. Since Tudor times the shallow waters have silted up considerably along this stretch of coast, dominated by the Isle of Sheppey, and whose fertility tempted the Danes to settle in England. At Whitstable, to the east, where the shore provided oysters for the Romans and still supplies the London markets, the sea begins to clear. Herne Bay, along the coast, is a seaside resort, as is Margate, the latter a big one in the traditional bright and breezy English manner. If you are looking for sugar or rubber false teeth, or salt and pepper sets in the shape of female breasts, this is the place to find them. Broadstairs, round the corner, is hardly less crowded than Margate in summer, but it has a slightly more discreet air, perhaps because of its association with Charles Dickens, who lived and worked there and whose presence is still celebrated each year by the Dickens Society.

Although Rye now stands back from the sea, to which its harbour is joined by a channel, the town still has a seafaring air and lovely old buildings. St. Mary's Church, which offers a fine panorama over the town, is Norman, and the Mermaid Inn, where pirates and smugglers often met, is early sixteenth century.

Ramsgate, down the coast a mile or so, faces the treacherous Goodwin Sands, graveyard of many ships, and its lighthouse flashes warnings echoed by the Goodwin lightships floating out at sea. Henry VIII built castles along this easily invaded coast: Deal is now a ruin but Walmer, still habitable, is the official residence of the Lords Warden of the Cinque Ports. The great Norman castle at Dover, within which are the foundations of a Roman lighthouse, still stands guard over the white cliffs. Though its harbour is artificial, Dover, with its neighbour Folkestone, is one of the busiest ports in Britain, dealing with millions of holiday travellers and a continual flow of juggernauts carrying freight and the produce of farms in France. Germany, Spain and Italy into Britain.

The Romney, Walland and Denge Marshes, which separate the ports from resorts farther west, are low-lying and at first sight look uninteresting, but they have a strange, eerie quality which smacks of ghosts and wild events. Indeed, this area, often covered in sea mists, was favoured by smugglers and others with a piratical turn of mind, and Rye, whose harbour now lies inland from the sea and is reached by a river, was a favourite rendezvous. Its closely packed old houses, clustering on the hump of a hill which once bordered the sea, still have all the seafaring atmosphere of 200 or more years ago. Running across the marshes parallel to the coast between Hythe and Dungeness is the miniature Romney Hythe and Dymchurch Light Railway, much patronized by holidaymakers, while at Dungeness itself the shape of things to come materializes in the forms of two nuclear power stations.

New Romney, the largest town on the Romney Marsh, was one of the medieval Cinque Ports, a defensive association of ports intended to be the country's first line of defence against the French. The original Cinque Ports, all of which received special privileges in return for their contribution to the defence of the coast, were Hastings, Romney, Hythe, Dover and Sandwich; Rye and Winchelsea were added to the association later.

Hastings is the most easterly of the major south-east coast resorts. Most of them began as fishing villages but, with the arrival of the railways in the nineteenth century, soon developed into playgrounds for the working classes especially from London, and summer residences for the better-off. In Hastings, these aspects are still very evident in the fishing village and fun fair at the eastern end and the Regency and Victorian houses stretching westwards towards St. Leonards.

Bexhill is another rather discreet resort, built by the Earl de la Warr, one of the resort developers of the nineteenth century. William the Conqueror landed at a beach between Hastings and Bexhill and the battle of Hastings, in which Harold lost his English kingdom and his life, was fought on the hills inland at the place now appropriately named Battle. Battle Abbey, built by William to celebrate his victory, was destroyed at the time of the dissolution of the monasteries by Henry VIII, but some vestiges remain in the present buildings of a girls' school.

Farther west, Eastbourne became a fashionable resort in George III's time, and was much developed by the nineteenth-century planners, most notably the Duke of Devonshire, who wanted it to be an elegant and well-mannered resort, which it still is. The front and gardens are immaculately maintained, and the facades of the hotels and apartment houses all gleam with fresh paint. In the centre of the promenade is a Martello tower, one of many built along the coast to ward off the Napoleonic invasion which never came.

From the western end of Eastbourne one can walk along the shore to Beachy Head, a sheer 540-foot (165-m) cliff of white chalk which attracts thousands of visitors and, sadly, not a few would-be suicides who throw themselves on to the rocks below, where a lonely lighthouse witnesses their unhappy end.

Brighton is the star of this resort-filled coast and still has the slightly roué air of the Prince Regent, who made it popular from the 1780s. His enduring monument is the Brighton Pavilion, an extraordinary flight of fancy transported, it would appear, from Samarkand by Aladdin's magic lamp. 'Prinny,' as he was sometimes called and whose spirit is admirably evoked by Rex Whistler in a

The South Downs end with dramatic suddenness at Beachy Head (540 feet/165 m). The lighthouse built at the foot of the cliff in 1902 replaced the earlier one on the clifftop.

painting to be seen in Brighton Museum, had a flair for appointing imaginative architects, among them Henry Holland, who built the Pavilion, and John Nash, who is responsible for some of London's most dramatic settings in Regent's Park.

Though the Pavilion epitomizes Brighton it does not sum it up. There is a great deal more to Brighton than simple oriental panache. On the seaward side of the Pavilion was the original fishing village of Brighthelmstone, now transformed into an entertaining pedestrian precinct, with the original old houses converted into antique shops, boutiques, restaurants, bookshops and other businesses designed to entrance the visitors. Along the front to the east as far as the new marina at Black Rock, rows of handsome Georgian houses, some converted into hotels, present one of the finest seaside fronts in Europe. There are two piers, though the West Pier is in a sad state of decay, and beyond the more easterly Palace Pier, the Volks electric railway, the first ever to run in Britain, is still going strong. To the west, Brighton merges with more sedate Hove, also a place full of fine buildings but without that devil-may-care air of its sister resort.

The coast becomes flatter now as it heads towards the low-lying shores of Selsey Bill past resorts like Worthing, Littlehampton and Bognor Regis, whose royal title was granted by George V, though legend has it that when asked later

George IV may not have been everyone's idea of a king but he had an eye for architecture. The Royal Pavilion, rebuilt for him in Oriental style by Nash, is an extravaganza that fits well with the panache of Britain's famous south coast resort.

Opposite: *Chichester has a fine Norman cathedral with a separate belfry, rare in Britain. The plan of the town betrays its Roman origins, and nearby at Fishbourne is the largest Roman building in Britain.*

whether he would care to convalesce again in the town the king said 'Bother, Bognor', or words to that effect.

Between Selsey Bill and Southampton Water the coast is low-lying with the land no more than a few feet above the tidal flats, which are glittering expanses of water on which the boats ride at high tide, and mud flats at low. Chichester queens it over the villages here, a superb town with a fine Norman cathedral, a modern theatre in-the-round and a social centre for the boating fraternity that gathers in the creeks and estuaries of the jig-saw coast.

There are fascinating villages all around; Bosham, where the future King Harold attended the local church before his ill-starred trip to France, still has a wonderful and ancient air with its wooden quayside, and at Fishbourne there are the ruins of a Roman palace with superb mosaic floors. From Birdham, at the entrance to Chichester harbour, the artist Turner painted the famous view which is in the picture collection at Petworth House.

Farther west, past the caravan camps of Hayling Island, lies the great naval base of Portsmouth, where Nelson's *Victory* – over which young sailors will guide you with lively descriptions of life aboard in Nelson's time – rests in dry dock. Nearby rests another great warship, Henry VIII's *Mary Rose*, sunk in Tudor times and now raised from its watery bed. Portsmouth suffered much damage during World War II, but enough remains of the old dockside to fill the imagination with images of the people who lined the quays when the great men-of-war came in. There is plenty of history here. The first Duke of Buckingham, favourite of Charles I, was killed at Portsmouth; Charles Dickens was born in Commercial Road; and on the hills above the port are four forts and buildings from which the invasion fleets of World War II were commanded.

The great liners that once filled Southampton Water are no longer to be seen in such crowds, but the great commercial dockyards still operate and there is still plenty of activity in the port. The city is large and prosperous and has a university and a fine maritime museum. On the west side of Southampton Water lies Fawley, a large oil refinery whose fiery night-time outline is a symbol of the industrialized world. Only just round the corner, on the Beaulieu River, Buckler's Hard seems almost unchanged since the times when the river shore was filled with ships that Henry Adams built for Nelson's fleet and which towered over the cottages of the tiny community. Nearby is Beaulieu Abbey, home of Lord Montagu, in whose grounds is the National Motor Museum.

The old world still survives strongly in the villages along the western Solent, the stretch of water which separates the Isle of Wight from the mainland. At Lymington, where yachts crowd the harbour, there are rows of Georgian houses and good eating places, and on the end of the spit of sand swept along the coast by the Channel tides is Henry VIII's Hurst Castle, in excellent condition and open daily to visitors.

Christchurch, on the estuary formed by the Avon River as it enters the sea at Hengistbury Head, also has an historic atmosphere, reinforced by the presence of the remains of a Norman castle and priory which can be visited. From the bridge you can watch the trout just as the monks did long ago. There is nothing pleasanter than to take a boat for a quiet sail or row around the wide river harbour surrounded by the green fields and woods of Hengistbury Head, a nature reserve.

Something of the wild woodlands of Hengistbury peninsula remains in the ravines, called chines, that tumble down to the sea in the great seaside city of Bournemouth. Though one of the last south coast resorts to be developed in the nineteenth century because it had no railway, Bournemouth grew very quickly. Its long beach, stretching to the east through the neighbouring resorts of Southbourne and Boscombe, and west to Poole Harbour, its pleasant weather and its proximity to the New Forest made it ideal for development, and now it has a vast number of entertainments, three piers, good shops and restaurants, while still retaining the sedate residential character of its early years.

With Brighton, which represents the stylish Regency period, and Margate, which began life as the workers' playground, Bournemouth represents an important chapter in the story of the development of English seaside resorts, which set a style in holidays that was to become a model for the whole world.

The Downs and the Weald

The North Downs of southern England stretch from East Kent to Hampshire, and a parallel range of South Downs runs from West Sussex to Beachy Head. Between them, in Kent, lies the Weald. The smooth, whale-backed downs are sparsely wooded and make good walking country, in which one can enjoy fine views of the wooded valleys with their rich farmlands and flint cottages and, here and there, massed unobtrusively, the roofs and spires of a country town.

Despite the traffic that crosses them heading for the Channel ports and the industry that has developed in the urban centres, the southern counties remain essentially rural, though most of those who live in their villages are more likely to be workers in London than in the adjoining fields. In this quiet landscape there remains plenty of evidence of the role played by the southern counties as the first line of defence against invasion and, later, as the playground of the rich and lordly, who preferred the warmer climate and richer pastures of the south to their more northern estates. Knights' houses and priories are still to be seen, and the Way trod by pilgrims making for the shrine of Thomas à Becket in Canterbury can still be followed. Numerous paths have been re-opened in this countryside, including the South Downs Way, which can be followed from Eastbourne on the coast to Beacon Hill, the Weald Way from Gravesend to Eastbourne, and the well-trodden North Downs Way, all of which provide the best of rural views of the countryside.

The focal point of the eastern end of the North Downs is Canterbury, whose cathedral was founded in AD 597 by St. Augustine. Around this early centre of Christianity grew the city, which still has sections of the medieval buildings that gathered round the old Saxon and Norman church. In the cathedral, the Norman element is visible in the magnificent crypt, above which rose the Gothic cathedral we now see. Today Canterbury is a fine town whose modern amenities attract day trippers from across the Channel as much as its splendid history. Surrounding the city are charming, unspoiled villages like Littlebourne, Patrixbourne, Chartham, and Chilham where there is a castle which contains a Battle of Britain museum.

To the west, Maidstone lies on the River Medway, which flows north to Chatham. This is an area rich in castles and country houses. Near Maidstone, medieval Leeds Castle, surrounded by its moat, is one of the most spectacular and beautiful. Sissinghurst, to the south in the Weald of Kent, is more a country house than a castle, and is famous for its wonderful garden, created by Vita Sackville-West and Sir Harold Nicolson, her husband. Another castle, Allington, is now incorporated into a school.

Above left: In summertime, poppies bloom beside the South Downs Way. A walkers' path, it follows an interesting route between Lewes and Eastbourne passing the Long Man of Wilmington, a mysterious figure cut out of the chalk hills, and Firle Beacon, one of the points from which threats to England by Spanish fleets were signalled to Queen Elizabeth's government.

Ightham Mote, a charming red-brick and timber building near Sevenoaks, is a near-perfect medieval house showing the transition from castle to manor house as life in England became more peaceful. It lies in a small wooded valley whose stream feeds the moat around the house. Also near Sevenoaks is Knole, a vast house set in a superb park and containing magnificent furniture, paintings and other riches. This is a lovely area of downland and farmland culminating in a splendid wooded spur of chalk hillside at Box Hill near Dorking. The Roman road called Stane Street runs under the High Street in Dorking, where the White Horse Inn was one of the hostelries patronized by Mr. Pickwick and his friends.

Between Guildford, with its steep High Steeet, splendid Angel Hotel, keep built by Henry II, modern university and cathedral, and Petworth, where medieval houses lie at the gates of Petworth House, the inspiration for many of Turner's later paintings, is the western edge of the Weald, the rich farming land that extends between the Downs.

The Weald is a garden landscape of woods, green fields and orchards, where, especially in Kent, apples flourish and where hop-picking was once a summer

Christ Church Gate is the main entrance to the cathedral precinct at Canterbury. St. Augustine founded both the abbey nearby and the cathedral. The latter became a great centre of pilgrimage after the murder of Thomas à Becket.

task for workers from London. It has always been a favoured area of England in which to live, so it is not surprising that great names abound. Daniel Defoe was a visitor to Royal Tunbridge Wells, a spa with a famous shopping terrace called the Pantiles, in the centre of the Kentish Weald, but he could not afford to stay; John Gay, composer of *The Beggar's Opera*, did. At nearby Penshurst Place, a noble house where Sir Philip Sidney was born, Ben Jonson was a frequent visitor. Anne Boleyn's family home was Hever Castle, and here she spent her childhood and teenage years. Winston Churchill's country home was Chartwell, near Westerham; Rudyard Kipling lived at Batemans, near Burwash in the Weald of East Sussex, and Conan Doyle at Crowborough, a few miles away to the north-east. There are also famous castles in this area: Scotney, at Lamberhurst; Bodiam, built to discourage French raiders up the Rother valley from Rye; and Herstmonceaux, now the Royal Observatory, at the northern end of the flat land stretching to Pevensey.

The South Downs are narrower and shorter than the North Downs, forming a splendid background to the coast between Chichester and Eastbourne. Their smooth, grass-covered slopes make good walking country and give birds'-eye views of expansive sweeps of the coast and English Channel. At their western end lies the Victorian town of Arundel, with its formidable castle looking over the River Arun. The castle, owned by the Dukes of Norfolk, Earls Marshal of England, was built by the Earl of Shrewsbury soon after William the Conqueror's arrival in England. Though it suffered under an attack from Cromwell's troops, it was rebuilt and now provides a superb spectacle for visitors, who may wander freely through the extensive castle parkland. The Arun runs down to Littlehampton, which once served as a port for France and an unloading place for Caen stone imported during Norman times for vast building projects.

One of the most attractively situated castles in southern Britain, Scotney is almost more a manor house than a castle, and the major part of it was built in the seventeenth century.

Up on the Downs behind the gleaming modern resorts is an older world where it is said the ghosts of Celts who built their forts at Chanctonbury Ring and Cissbury Ring still haunt the woods at night. Both forts can be reached on foot from the road from Worthing, and there are glorious views from the downland hilltops which the Celts defended against the Saxon invaders. Another summit worth ascending is that of Ditchling Beacon, 813 feet (248 m) high with extensive views over the Weald. The South Downs Way passes by here, and on its route, at Clayton, are two remaining windmills of the hundreds that once caught the westerly breezes off the Channel.

The beacons were England's early warning system of Tudor times; their light, passing from hilltop to hilltop, alerted the English defences to the approach of hostile ships. The one at Firle behind Beachy Head must have blazed when the Spanish Armada was driven up the Channel by Drake and Effingham in 1588, and it is worth taking the mile walk to it from the road near West Firle to let the setting stir the images of those dramatic days. From the beacon one can look down over the Glynde valley in which summer opera flourishes at Glyndebourne. Not far away the Glynde joins the River Ouse after it passes the old county town of Lewes, a treasure house of Georgian buildings, old inns and a castle.

Before the South Downs plunge into the sea at Beachy Head they pass through Wilmington, a small village near Eastbourne, above which a mysterious figure is cut in the chalk slopes of Windover Hill. This is the Long Man of Wilmington, a 231-foot (70-m) male figure holding a staff in each hand. No one knows his origin but Stone and Bronze Age relics have been dug up on the hill. Whatever he is or whenever he was made, the Long Man of Wilmington is a potent symbol still, representing the enigmatic side of the smiling countryside which has developed on the billions of sea animals which formed the chalk strata on the sea-bed aeons ago.

The Hampshire Basin

Some of the most beautiful rivers in England drain down through the woods of the great basin formed by the Downs to the east, the Marlborough Downs and Salisbury Plain to the north and the hills of Dorsetshire to the west. They are not large rivers, but their banks are wooded and they flow swiftly, rippling over stony beds or gliding smoothly over fronds of green river weeds among which chub, perch, pike and trout hide.

In the east, the River Test flows down into Southampton, the Meon travels down the lovely and unspoiled Meon valley, and the Avon, beginning its journey far away in the Vale of Pewsey north of Salisbury Plain, joins the sea at Christchurch. One of its tributaries flowing from the Somerset border meets it at Christchurch harbour.

This well-watered land of hills and valleys is exuberantly green and fertile, perhaps the reason why King Alfred made it the centre of his kingdom of Wessex, with its capital at Winchester. The Norman kings moved their capital to London, but continued to frequent Winchester, where Parliament met, and it was William the Conqueror who turned the New Forest into a hunting preserve.

Winchester has been a cathedral place since Saxon times, and its 556-foot-long (170-m) Norman cathedral sits solidly in the centre of the city in a beautiful walled precinct with lawns and houses whose architecture ranges over medieval, seventeenth-century and Georgian styles. There is little left of the walls that once surrounded the city, though Kingsgate remains as one of the entrances to the

Right: Broadlands was the home of Lord Mountbatten and is situated near Romsey north of Southampton. It was formerly the home of Lord Palmerston, one of Queen Victoria's prime ministers.

cathedral precinct and Westgate is in the centre of the town by the Castle Hall, built by Henry III on the remains of the Norman castle.

The River Itchen, which flows through Winchester, has many pretty villages and country houses in its valley, including Avington House, where Nell Gwynne lived for a while, and Twyford House, which Benjamin Franklin visited.

The Test, which, like the Itchen, flows into Southampton Water, is one of the best trout-fishing rivers in England with Stockbridge as a recognized centre for the sport. Near the town is Marsh Court, a house built by the architect Sir Edwin Lutyens. Among the many enchanting villages along the banks of the Test and its tributaries are the quaintly named Wallops – Over, Nether and Middle – where old cottages, many of them thatched, hide among the trees of the Wallop valley.

As the Test approaches Southampton Water it passes through Romsey, a town inhabited by the Saxons and possessing a fine Norman abbey. Broadlands, the home of the late Earl Mountbatten of Burma, is nearby. Another lovely valley near Southampton Water is that of the Meon River, which reaches the Solent west of Fareham and Gosport. The A32 traces the up-river course of the Meon north towards Alton, bringing two famous villages near this pleasant market town within each reach of literary pilgrims. The village are Chawton, where the cottage in which Jane Austen lived with her family and wrote most of her novels, is now lovingly preserved, and Selborne, home and inspiration of the naturalist Gilbert White. The house in which he died, The Wakes, contains a Gilbert White museum and a small memorial museum on Captain Oates, the Antarctic explorer who died on the ill-fated 1912 Scott expedition.

The longest river in the Hampshire Basin is the Avon, which begins its life in the Marlborough Downs, passing through Salisbury Plain and by Amesbury, near which lies the ancient Druidical monument of Stonehenge. This vast circle of stones, the tallest of which is 21 feet (6½ m) high, has been the source of much speculation over the centuries, but no one knows precisely the reason for its existence. Its importance to its builders is testified to by the fact that some of the stones for its construction were brought from as far away as Wales. Though its

Below: The standing stones of Stonehenge on Salisbury Plain are something of a mystery. Some of the stones were brought from as far away as Wales, and the purpose of the monument is thought to be connected with sun-worship as the midsummer sun rises over the Hele Stone, the axis-point of the circle.

significance is perhaps of small importance to us today, there is no doubt that its mystery remains and exerts a powerful attraction on the hundreds of visitors who see it each year and on those who attend the midsummer ceremonies performed there every year by the Most Ancient Order of Druids.

A little farther south the Avon flows through Salisbury, whose cathedral with its soaring 404-foot (123-m) spire is universally known through the paintings of John Constable. Salisbury was built where the Bourne, the Nadder and the Wylye join the Avon, at first on the hill to the north, where the Norman ruins of Old Sarum can still be seen, and in 1220 on the site where it stands today. The Cathedral Close gives a perfect image of the medieval world with its wide-open spaces and thirteenth-century houses, such as the Bishop's Palace and the Deanery. Around the Close there are also many old half-timbered houses and two fourteenth-century inns, the Haunch of Venison and the Rose and Crown. The city's ideal situation and fertile valleys encouraged the building of great mansions in the countryside around. Among these are Trafalgar House at Alderbury, given to Nelson's family after his death; Longford Castle to the south, and Wilton House on the banks of the River Nadder, built on the site of an abbey and rebuilt by Inigo Jones; Little Clarendon, a Tudor manor house near the village of Dinton, which also boasts Phillips House and Lawes Cottage, the latter the home of John Lawes, composer and friend of Milton.

Constable painted this view of Salisbury Cathedral, architecturally the most unified of all the English cathedrals. It was started in 1220 and completed in 1258, with the spire added in the fourteenth century, and sits in a handsome close with fine old houses.

The New Forest in Hampshire was William the Conqueror's hunting ground and is still the home of wild deer, and of the ubiquitous New Forest ponies. In its centre is Lyndhurst, where the Alice of Lewis Carroll's books is buried.

The Avon's splendid journey south to the English Channel finishes in a burst of glory as it wends its way through the western edge of the New Forest. This former royal hunting ground, where to shoot a king's deer meant death and where William Rufus was killed by an arrow shot by Walter Tyrrell, is one of the most beautiful forests in England. Ancient oaks, giant conifers, beeches and ash grow to splendid proportions in the sheltered areas, and on the higher land there are wild moorlands. Ringwood, on the river, is a trout-fishing centre; it was here that the Duke of Monmouth, natural son of Charles II, was brought a prisoner after his abortive rebellion against James II. Lyndhurst and Brockenhurst, in the centre of the forest, are both charming old towns. Alice Liddell, the original Alice in Wonderland, is buried in the cemetery at Lyndhurst.

The forest is popular riding country. Herds of sturdy New Forest ponies wander at will, as do deer and other wilder animals, though they are seldom seen, except by walkers along the forest paths, including the fifteen walks laid out by the Forestry Commission through various parts of the forest.

The Isle of Wight

Only a few miles separate the Isle of Wight from the mainland embarcation points of Portsmouth, Southampton and Lymington, but they are enough to give the island a different character. The cost and time of the crossing has created a separate community on the island, increased in summertime by weekend visitors and especially by people who keep their boats at the various island harbours. Except for the major resorts on the south-east side, this has enabled the island to preserve a rural atmosphere that is part of its charm.

Cowes, at the northernmost tip, is the internationally famous island town where the annual yachting regatta takes place. During Cowes Week the terraced streets of the town grow lively with the international sailing set, and the Solent gleams with the slivers of a thousand sails. At other times of the year Cowes is a quiet place. The River Medina, which reaches inland to Newport, divides the town into East Cowes, with its boat yards, hovercraft works and other light industries, and West Cowes. Queen Victoria and Prince Albert liked the town and built Osborne House, an opulent Italian-style mansion, above East Cowes, where the bathing machine from which the queen took her first step into the sea is still preserved.

To the east of Cowes lies Ryde, which possesses a half-mile-long (800-m) pier on which runs an electric railway, the only one on the island, to ferry visitors to the seaside resorts on the east coast. There is a splendid view of Ryde from the end of the pier at which the passenger ferries from Portsmouth dock. From here the largely Victorian and Edwardian houses of the town can be seen rising to the crest of the hill. The front is typical of English seaside resorts, with gardens, ponds, fairgrounds, amusement arcades and a good, sandy beach.

On the most easterly point of the island is Bembridge, once the mouth of Brading harbour but now silted up. This is where the ships of Nelson's day used to shelter from the west winds and where today heron and other marsh birds feed among the often flooded fields. Bembridge School, a public school on the outskirts of the town, contains a fine collection of the works of John Ruskin.

The attractive village of Brading now lies inland on the road from Ryde to Sandown and Shanklin. These two resorts, which accommodate the major part of the Isle of Wight's summer holiday-makers, still preserve an Edwardian air with their small stone houses and neat gardens. Both have good beaches and Shanklin has an older part of the town with thatched cottages, tea rooms, and one of those gardens in a ravine, or chine, created by romantic Victorians and still giving much pleasure today.

The chalk cliffs rise sharply to the south of Shanklin, and the wooded and secluded village of Bonchurch clings to the steep slopes below the main road. Immediately adjoining it is Ventnor, a charming place built on an amphitheatre of terraced cliffs which surround the bay, in which a small pier completes the Edwardian scene. Above the town rises the St. Boniface Down, at 787 feet (240 m) the highest point on the Isle of Wight.

The south coast of the island is most attractive, with cliffs and downland over which hang-gliders are often seen hovering. St. Catherine's Point is the most southerly point of the island and a dangerous place for boats and bathers, though

Overleaf: The chalk stacks stretching out to sea from the south-west corner of the Isle of Wight and known as the Needles are a popular visitors' attraction. So are the multicoloured sands of Alum Bay, which are used to create pictures or bottled in stratified layers.

Shanklin, on the Isle of Wight, is a popular summer resort with an old-world corner with thatched houses on its upper level and a good beach, pier and busy esplanade by the sea. Keats and Longfellow both stayed here.

On the west side of the Isle of Wight is the attractive little yachting centre of Yarmouth. Henry VIII built one of his south coast castles here, looking across the entrance of the Solent to Lymington on the mainland.

popular with sightseers, who visit the lighthouse or the tiny fishing harbour at Castle Haven or walk down to the shore through the Blackgang Chine to the west.

The road keeps to the cliff tops above the sea along this section of coast, giving fine views of the English Channel; at its western end is Freshwater Bay, a popular bathing place surrounded by cliffs and within walking distance over the grassy cliff top to the Needles, a famous series of chalk stacks which march out to sea at the mouth of the Solent. On the north side of the Needles is Alum Bay, famed for its multicoloured cliffs whose sands gave rise to the art of sand picture-making.

Past the wooded village of Totland farther north lies West Wight's largest harbour, at Yarmouth, where the River Yar provides moorings and anchorage

for hundreds of pleasure boats and a port for the ferry from Lymington. The village of Yarmouth is well maintained and includes a small castle built by Henry VIII. Newton which lies between Yarmouth and Cowes is another popular anchorage for boats, but there is no town here, and the estuary, which is pretty and unspoiled and a sanctuary for birds, is under the care of the National Trust.

Despite its small size, the Isle of Wight has much variety. A spine of chalk hills running across its centre gives splendid views over the entire island, and on these slopes there are pretty farms, picture-postcard villages like Godshill, and even a vineyard. At Carisbrooke, near Newport, the island's capital, there is a splendid castle, built on the site of a fort established by the Romans, who called the island Vectis. Charles I and two of his children were imprisoned in Carisbrooke Castle during the Civil War period and the Interregnum.

The
Thames Valley

The River Thames, running 209 miles (336 km) from its source near Cirencester in Gloucestershire to the North Sea, was the great waterway of England even in Roman times, which is why the Romans developed an extensive port, now being unearthed by archaeologists, in London. Passage up the Thames must have involved a good deal of porterage where today's weirs and locks, perfectly maintained by the Thames Conservancy, control the flow of water, but it gave access to area of commercial and agricultural importance as well as providing a highway for the troops who controlled the subject populations. The Romans built many of the fords and bridges across the Thames and founded towns near them.

Since then, the Thames has continued to grow in commercial value, coming to its most important period as a commercial waterway, linked by canal to the Midlands, in the nineteenth century. Because of this, one has to consider the Thames Valley and its tributary valleys as a whole, a region west of the great London conurbation, whose spinal chord is the great river which has inspired more political rivalry and more poetry than perhaps any other on earth.

The 'Valley' section of the Thames may be said to be that part which lies upstream from where the tidal river of metropolitan London becomes the non-

Among the green fields that border the River Thames between Windsor and Burnham is the tiny village of Dorney. Its old brick Tudor houses include 'Prior's Croft', seen here, and it has a medieval church.

tidal river – upstream, that is, from Richmond-upon-Thames and Teddington Lock. Even here, the river banks are, with some exceptions, suburban in character, and it is not until one is past Hampton Court Palace and almost at Windsor that they take on a rural aspect.

The rural section of the Thames has its eastern end in Berkshire, just below Windsor at Runnymede. In a field near the river here, the first political triumph for what was to become parliamentary rule took place when the barons obliged King John to sign Magna Carta. The river's banks at Windsor Great Park are also green and tree-lined, but one feels that there is something artificial, planned perhaps by a Capability Brown, about them.

The real countryside begins upstream beyond Maidenhead, where a lovely bridge by Isambard Kingdom Brunel spans the river. The town was a popular rendezvous for Edwardian dandies whose punts crowded Boulter's Lock, now full on summer Sundays with the motor boats of London commuters. After Boulter's Lock there are miles of fields, water meadows and beech-covered hillsides, above which stands Cliveden, a grand Italian-style house surrounded by elegant gardens and a park built on the site of a house once owned by Charles I's favourite, the Duke of Buckingham. The views from the terrace over the formal parterre to the river are among the best in the lower Thames Valley, and must have been enjoyed by many of Britain's leading politicians when Nancy, Lady Astor, gave her celebrated parties for the 'Cliveden Set' here in the 1930s.

Above Cliveden Reach, through which the weekend tourist steamers and hired cruisers ply their sluggish way, there comes the first of many famous Thames-side villages. Cookham has a long, narrow street of houses, many of them half-timbered, and a bridge over the river that anyone with a knowledge of the work of Stanley Spencer, perhaps the most original English artist of this century, will instantly recognize. There is a Stanley Spencer Museum in the High Street, and his painting *The Last Supper* hangs in the charming twelfth-century church by the river.

At Marlow, upriver from Cookham, and just within Buckinghamshire, there is another riverside church, nineteenth-century this time, and a tumultuous weir overlooked by an elegant white suspension bridge built in 1832, and a fine hotel,

Marlow, which lies on the River Thames between Maidenhead and Henley, is a pretty town with a large weir, a riverside church and a suspension bridge. It is a popular centre for boating enthusiasts.

Overleaf: Hambleden Mill is by the River Thames on the Marlow-Henley Road. The attractive village of Hambleden lies a quarter of a mile (400 m) inland and has a fine old church.

the Compleat Angler, named after Izaak Walton's book, though it is not certain that the famous fisherman ever stayed there. A book that did get written in Marlow was Mary Shelley's *Frankenstein*, in a house which still stands in West Street. Above Marlow on the southern bank of the river are the wooded slopes of Quarry Wood, which Kenneth Graham used as the model for his Wild Wood in *The Wind in the Willows*.

This north-looping stretch of the river, between Maidenhead and Henley, and marked by villages whose churches, tithe barns and ancient, low-beamed pubs attest to centuries of occupation, has inspired other writers too, notably Jerome K. Jerome whose *Three Men in a Boat* got themselves into various kinds of trouble on the river. At Hambleden, upstream from Marlow, is another great weir, much used by whitewater canoeists as a practice run, and an attractive old weatherboard mill recently converted into apartments.

Henley-on-Thames, lying on the left (or Oxfordshire) bank of the river, comes to its annual moment of glory every July when the international Henley Royal Regatta takes place. But it is a fine, busy town in its own right, with a twelfth-century church, a handsome eighteenth-century bridge and several pubs whose ages span the centuries. Upriver, the land to either side is wonderfully tranquil with, here and there, the well-manicured lawns of some country house spreading out along the tree-clad river banks, often dotted with charmingly eccentric summer houses or boat sheds. It is rather as if Edwardian England were still alive and well and taking tea along the Thames.

At Reading, the rural atmosphere recedes as the Thames flows through the university town which is also a busy commercial centre, but it returns almost immediately as the river, coming south from Oxford, traces one of the loveliest parts of its journey. Pangbourne, Goring and, on the opposite bank, Streatley all lie along the banks of the river as one cruises north past the western end of the Chilterns. Once again one is in a part of rural England whose quiet beauty seems to have lasted from an earlier age – an impression reinforced by a visit to Basildon Park, near Pangbourne, whose Georgian elegance, seen in both the house designed by John Carr and the park, has been finely restored in recent times.

Wallingford, farther upstream, has always been an important Thames crossing-point and in the Civil War was the last Royalist town to fall to Cromwell's forces. In the thirteenth century a bridge replaced the ford and provides a way across the river even today. To the east lies Ewelme, a pretty little village where Henry VIII honeymooned with his fifth wife, Catherine Howard. Elizabeth I also used Ewelme as a country retreat, as had Chaucer's granddaughter Alice, who married the Earl of Suffolk and during whose lifetime were built the fifteenth-century church, school and almshouses which may still be seen today.

Upstream the Thames is joined by the Thame, on whose banks lies Dorchester – not the Dorset town, but the descendant of yet another Roman camp, though what one sees today owes its appearance to medieval and eighteenth-century architects, rather than the Romans. Half-timbered houses add to the attractions of the High Street, the old Roman Road, and to the south of the town is one of the finest abbeys to be found along the Thames. A Norman building with fourteenth-century glass windows, it has a remarkable lych gate built in the nineteenth century and a gabled structure built in the fourteenth century as the village school.

The land to the west of the Thames takes its character from the Berkshire and Lambourn Downs, in whose folds lie many old villages and not a few horse-training establishments, and the Vale of the White Horse, watered by the River Ock, which flows into the Thames at Abingdon. The date and origins of the stylized figure of the horse cut into the white chalk at Uffington, which gives the vale its name, is unknown, though it may date from around 100 BC. The 374-foot (114-m) figure on the side of White Horse Hill can be reached by a path from the village. Farther up the hill is Uffington Castle, on the Ridgeway, an ancient path which originally ran across southern England from Devon to the Wash, and which still provides splendid walking for many miles. Wantage, the birthplace of Alfred the Great, whose statue stands in the main square, is the largest town in the Vale of the White Horse.

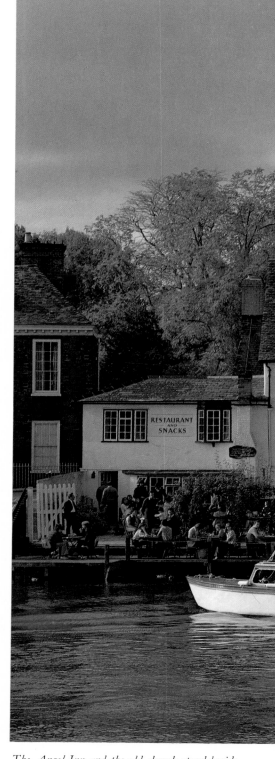

The Angel Inn and the old church stand beside the bridge over the river at Henley-on-Thames. Henley is at its most animated in July during Royal Regatta week, but the attractive Thameside town, set amid wooded hills, is popular with visitors all summer.

Abingdon, at the junction of the Ock and the Thames, has existed as a Thames-side town certainly since the seventh century, when the Benedictine abbey, whose ruins can be seen along the river, was founded. The church of St. Nicholas is twelfth century, and there are several other buildings which date back to medieval times, though the town also has interesting buildings of later times, including the County Hall and Guildhall.

A few miles upstream, the Thames, here called the Isis, skirts the western side of the great university city of Oxford, whose spires, pinnacles, domes and turrets dominate the skyline from several miles away. The university, begun in the twelfth century, soon attracted scholars from all over Europe, and a number of the 34 colleges and 5 halls one sees today, among them Balliol, Merton, New, University College and St. Edmund Hall, date from the thirteenth century. Off the main streets of the busy, industrial city which Oxford is today it is still possible to recapture some of the medieval atmosphere of the town and to imagine the life of the university at a period when Europe was just emerging from centuries of intellectual neglect.

As in Cambridge, the river and its main tributary, the Cherwell, plays a big part in the life of the university, though unlike Cambridge, Oxford's colleges lie away from the rivers in the town centre. Below Folly Bridge, on the main Abingdon Road at Christ Church Meadow, the college barges and boat houses are sited, and it is here, on Eights Reach, that the College eights compete energetically in the summer term. The elegant and leisurely pursuit of punting is very much the preserve of the lovely willow-edged Cherwell, with Magdalen Bridge the place to hire one's punt, canoe or rowing boat.

Among the glories of Oxford is the Bodleian Library and its attendant reading room, the circular, domed Radcliffe Camera. The Bodleian, named after the Elizabethan diplomat Sir Thomas Bodley, who restored Oxford's scattered medieval library between 1598 and 1613, contains over three million volumes and is one of the world's leading libraries.

Another interesting place is the thirteenth-century church of St. Mary the Virgin, where Thomas Cranmer, Nicholas Ridley and Hugh Latimer were all tried and condemned to death during Mary Tudor's reign for their support of the Protestant Reformation. The Martyrs' Memorial in St. Giles was erected to their memory in 1841–3, and a cross in the roadway in Broad Street marks where Latimer and Ridley were burnt at the stake in 1555. Christ Church, projected by Cardinal Wolsey in 1525 and established by Henry VIII in 1546, was Charles I's headquarters during the Civil War. The bell known as Great Tom, after Thomas à Becket, rang out the curfew every evening from its tower, built by Sir Christopher Wren, and which dominates St. Aldates and Tom Quad, Oxford's largest quadrangle.

Upstream from Oxford, the Thames sweeps along the edge of the Cotswolds past Cricklade, the upper limit for navigation. Above here, the great river is a narrow stream, growing out of the bare trickle which it is at its source at Thameshead near Cirencester.

Tom Tower, in St. Aldate Street, Oxford, stands at the entrance to Christ Church and houses the bell called Great Tom, whose tolling once signalled the closing of the university's gates each evening.

The Chilterns

The chalk hills that stretch across England from Goring Gap, through which the Thames flows between Oxford and Henley, to St. Albans in Hertfordshire make up a region of rural countryside where beechwoods alternate with farmlands and rounded grassy hilltops where sheep quietly graze. Despite the growth of commuter towns in this region close to London, many of its villages remain little touched by modern development, and much of the countryside is protected from over-development. The River Thame, which joins the Thames at Abingdon, marks the northern edge of the Chilterns, and its wide valley, leading to Aylesbury, provides good views for walkers using the Ridgeway along the hills.

Many of the Chilterns' prettiest and least-changed villages lie in the countryside around High Wycombe, once a picturesque market town and now a busy commercial centre, with all the usual concrete shopping precincts and giant supermarkets that modern commerce seems sadly to encourage. Of the few old buildings remaining to give the town character, the parish church, dating from the thirteenth to sixteenth centuries, and standing on its green island amid the shops and traffic, is outstanding. The eighteenth-century Guildhall and Market House sit amid market stalls in a section of the town being restored with some sympathy. West of the town is West Wycombe Park, a superb Palladian mansion rebuilt by the Dashwoods, whose most colourful ancestor was the eighteenth-century Sir Francis Dashwood who founded the Hell Fire Club. The artificial caves where the club conducted its gambling and drinking orgies are by the grounds of the splendid park, designed by Capability Brown, and now a National Trust property. The Hell Fire Club also used to conduct its orgies at Medmenham Abbey, on the Thames above Marlow.

North of High Wycombe is Hughenden Manor, country home of Benjamin Disraeli, Earl of Beaconsfield. The ornate but domestic atmosphere of this attractive house, lovingly maintained by the National Trust, gives visitors an insight into the character of this remarkable British statesman.

Among the many other villages within reach of this part of the Chilterns are Princes Risborough and Monks Risborough, both near the old Icknield Way,

part of the Ridgeway Path and a right-of-way since prehistoric times; Great Missenden and Little Missenden; and, totally isolated from the more prosaic aspects of modern life, such villages as Fingest, Frieth and Turville, which have a rustic simplicity, fine medieval churches and good pubs.

Beaconsfield, east of High Wycombe on the main London road, is an attractive and busy village, particularly in its older parts along the High Street, and though sometimes much visited at weekends, it manages to preserve its character. Among its various attractions are Bekonscot Model Village, and Burnham Beeches, a beautiful stretch of woodland.

Amersham, which lies nearer London and is connected to it by the Underground Metropolitan line, has a modern part on the hill and a lovely old town below. Here, the long broad high street of timber and brick houses and Georgian mansions gives a good picture of eighteenth-century England. Many of the well-preserved buildings are antique shops, craft shops and restaurants and there are several interesting pubs.

To the south-east of Amersham other attractive villages are to be found, though many now show signs of their role as commuter residential areas as new house estates are built. The Chalfonts – St. Giles and St. Peter – are here; Chalfont St. Giles preserves the cottage in which John Milton lived, and where he wrote his later work.

Farther east, the Chilterns become part of the green belt which surrounds London and which is a battlefield for those who wish to preserve England's countryside and those who wish to develop new residential estates for home-hungry Londoners. Amid the green landscapes of the Hertfordshire Chilterns, where the countryside is criss-crossed with rights-of-way providing walks for those who wish to explore on foot, is Whipsnade, the open-space part of the Zoological Gardens in London. Here wild animals roam in comparative freedom.

Bradenham Woods spread over the Chiltern Hills north-west of High Wycombe. Near them, at West Wycombe, is the home of the Dashwood family and the caves where Sir Francis Dashwood and his friends formed the Hell Fire Club.

One of the most elegant towns of western England is Cheltenham. The eighteenth- and nineteenth-century houses were built when Cheltenham was a fashionable spa, and many of them today serve as hotels for visitors to the many cultural festivals.

The Cotswolds

Perhaps no hills in England awake such feelings of affection and tenderness as do the Cotswolds of Gloucestershire and Oxfordshire. There is something about the little villages which stretch from Wotton-under-Edge in the south almost to Stratford-upon-Avon at the northern end, something about the honey-coloured stone houses, the churches – many of them magnificent monuments to the wealth of the wool merchants – the old farm buildings, the beechwoods and tidy hedgerows that humanizes the landscape and arouses deep sentiments in every visitor. There is nothing grand about the countryside here, nothing to inspire awe, but written across the landscape is the story of people who, since Anglo-Saxons first began to raise sheep here and gave the hills their name ('cot' means sheepfold), have built up a very personal and caring relationship with the land.

On their western edge the Cotswolds slope down sharply towards Gloucester and the Vale of Evesham; to the east they have a gentler slope, the hills merging gently with the valleys to which they descend; and to the south they are bordered by the valleys of the Thames and the Thame all the way to Aylesbury.

To the north along the Severn valley lies Gloucester, a bustling commercial town with a beautiful cathedral. In their northwards march the Cotswolds rise to some of their highest points; at Crickley Hill, where there is a Nature Park, and at Birdlip Hill there are fine views of the Vale of Gloucester with the Welsh mountains beyond, and at Cleeve Hill the land rises over 1,000 feet (305 m).

Cheltenham, once a fashionable spa and still an extremely elegant town with many streets of fine buildings and two highly regarded public schools, is just

The market square at Minchinhampton, near Stroud, is surrounded by honey-coloured stone houses typical of the Cotswold Hills. Like so many Cotswold villages, Minchinhampton was built largely by successful wool merchants.

below Cleeve Hill. The spa waters may still be taken at the Pump Room and one can still walk along the tree-lined Promenade as did the Regency bucks who frequented the town in the early nineteenth century. Cheltenham attracts visitors today because it is a fine town and because it is renowned for its festivals, which cover drama, dancing, music and literature and bring competitors from every part of the world.

It is in this area, to the south and east of Gloucester and Cheltenham, that one may find some of the finest of the Cotswold 'wool' churches, so called because they were built by wealthy woolstaplers, anxious to put at least a part of their wealth into works of piety and charity. There are almost a hundred of these medieval churches in the Cotswolds, probably the finest being at Burford, Cirencester, Chipping Campden, Fairford, Northleach and Winchcombe. Each of these possesses features of architectural and decorative beauty, especially monumental brasses and stained glass, to repay frequent visits.

To the north-east lie some of the loveliest of Cotswolds villages. Stow-on-the-Wold, perched on its hilltop and allegedly called 'the place where the wind blows cold', though there is little sign of it in summer, has many old cottages clustered round the market place and up its narrow streets. Bourton-on-the-Water is another enchanting place, where the River Windrush flows through the main street. Near Chipping Campden, in the far north of Gloucestershire, there is an added attraction in the bewitching gardens of Hidcote Manor, created early this century in 10 acres (4 hectares) of land on the Cotswold escarpment by Major Lawrence Johnston, who made it into a personal work of art.

Broadway, nearby, is perhaps the best-known of Cotswold villages, featuring in almost every tourist itinerary. Almost too good to be true, the lovely, immaculately kept village, with its creamy stone houses, also has one of the best-known pubs in England – if the word 'pub' can be used of such an elegantly old-world hotel. This is the Lygon Arms, before which the local hunt meets in winter to give a final touch to this most traditional of English scenes. Broadway

The seventeenth-century Market Hall at Chipping Campden stands in the centre of the broad High Street, like the Town Hall and Wool Staplers Hall. The name 'Chipping' comes from an old word meaning 'market' and refers to the important role of the village in the local wool trade.

Hill, 1,024 feet high (312 m), lies behind the village and has an eighteenth-century folly built for the Earl of Coventry. On a fine day, one is supposed to be able to see over a dozen counties from this viewpoint.

In north Oxfordshire, the manor houses in the Cotswold villages are often grander than those to the east, for it was in this rich land between Oxford and Stratford-upon-Avon that the rich wool merchants built their homes, many of which remain today. At Chastleton, a village with numerous thatched cottages, the manor house in Cotswold stone is of the Jacobean period, and near Banbury the moated manor house is fourteenth century. Burford, on the River Windrush,

Above: Bibury is on the River Coln north-east of Cirencester. Beside a mill stream which runs into the river is a group of seventeenth-century stone cottages known as Arlington Row. They were lived in by workers at Arlington Mill.

has a whole street of fine houses, fifteenth-century inns, a priory and the fine church of St. John the Baptist.

Grandest of all the houses in the southern foothills of the Cotswolds is Blenheim Palace, at Woodstock. This Baroque-style building by Vanbrugh was built between 1705 and 1715 for John Churchill, Duke of Marlborough, as a gift from a grateful queen and country to the successful general, and many famous artists were employed in its interior decoration, including Sir James Thornhill the painter, and Grinling Gibbons the woodworker. Sir Winston Churchill was born here and is buried in Bladon churchyard, a few miles away.

Overleaf: John Churchill, Duke of Marlborough, was given the manor house at Woodstock, near Oxford, in 1704 for his victory at Blenheim. The following year, he engaged Sir John Vanbrugh to create the splendid palace one sees today, and where Winston Churchill was born in 1874.

The South-West

In the south-west of England, that long, tapering peninsula striding out into the Atlantic as far as Land's End, the traveller is constantly aware of the drama of the landscape. Rugged cliffs, moorlands and heaths, chalk and limestone escarpments, granite rocks and wind-blown trees contrast sharply with sheltered valleys, where farms are laid out in neat checkerboard patterns and woods and copses nestle comfortably between the hills. This is a land which can be swept by Atlantic gales, and where along the coasts, the sea mists sometimes create a ghostly and mysterious world which breeds wild imaginings. In summer, it is a land of more sunshine than most parts of England, with coasts that are a kaleidoscope of colour created by the millions of holidaymakers who cluster along the beaches like migrant birds.

The south-west is a part of England relatively untouched by modern industrial development. The Phoenicians exploited the tin and clay deposits in Cornwall as did the Romans, and in the great age of exploration from Elizabethan to Victorian times the south-west ports were busy fitting up and crewing the ships that gained England the supremacy of the seas and also receiving the products of the new-found empire. Sugar and tobacco from the West Indies, cotton, hides and timber from America, tea and spices from the East, and human cargoes from Africa all passed through the south-west and western ports of England, making some of them – Bristol, for instance – into rich and elegant cities. But as the trade grew, traders began to look around for larger harbours nearer the great centres of population, and the ports of the west remained small or declined. The population, therefore, did not make the transition from pioneer to merchant, and the rugged individualism of the local character was not submerged in the uniformity of attitudes generally bred by conurbations.

Conservatism and independence of thought are the paradoxical characteristics of the south-west, which may explain why this part of England stood staunchly behind King Charles during the Civil War. It also helps to explain why the tourist development of recent years has not been allowed to change the character of the landscape or the people.

Except for the great motorway extending from London, Birmingham and the north down to Exeter and continuing as a dual highway to Plymouth, most of the roads in the south-west were built in the days of the horse and cart and, though mostly perfectly adequate for motor cars, do not encourage excessive speed. There has also been, except for one of two large resorts like Torquay and Newquay, no attempt to create holiday cities. All this makes the south-west an exceptional place for holidays – too much so, perhaps, in July and August when overcrowding of beaches, small towns, camp sites, and elsewhere becomes the norm. During the rest of the year, it is undoubtedly one of the most attractive parts of England, the fact that palm trees grow along the sea fronts saying something for the mildness of its climate.

There are many picturesque villages and hamlets throughout the West Country, the older buildings being made from local materials. In some parts a lack of slate led to the use of thatching, and, in places where the rock was unsuitable for building, a mixture of mud, straw and pebbles, called cob, was used instead.

Around the Coast from Poole to Bristol

The Isle of Purbeck, actually a peninsula, lies four-square to the south of Bournemouth and Poole Harbour, its precipitous chalk and limestone cliffs, backed by grassy downs, falling abruptly into the Channel and giving a taste of the landscape to come as one journeys towards the western tip of England. Swanage, where King Alfred defeated a Danish fleet in 877, is the Isle's beach resort and has an attractive setting, though for English picturesqueness at its best one should drive the few miles inland to the centre of the Isle to Corfe Castle. This pretty village of grey-stone houses and cottages is dominated by the dramatic outline of the castle itself, which was destroyed by Cromwell's troops after it had been defended for six weeks against a vastly superior Parliamentarian force by the Royalist Lady Bankes.

Left: Corfe Castle, in Dorset, rises above the village of stone houses like a stage set. It was blown up by Cromwell's troops after spirited resistance by the defenders. The castle, which is of Norman origin, dominates a gap in the Purbeck Hills.

Above: The great chalk cliff called Bat's Head lies near Durdle Door, a natural chalk arch standing out to sea. These coastal wonders are near Lulworth Cove, a bay almost totally enclosed by sheer white cliffs.

Farther west, after its initial bravura, the Dorset coast subsides into the calm flat stretch of the Chesil Bank, a curious shingle reef which extends out into the Channel to the Isle of Portland and westward to Abbotsbury. Here descendants of the swans first introduced by the monks who built the Benedictine abbey breed and preen themselves in the largest swannery in England. The village is charming and has a long line of cottages, many of them thatched, as well as the old monastery garden in which sub-tropical plants flourish. Beyond Abbotsbury the coast begins to rise again, reaching a summit, enjoyed by walkers along the Dorset Coast Path, at Golden Cap, at 617 feet (188 m) the tallest cliff along the south coast of England.

Lyme Regis is a charming little town, set in a gap in the cliffs, and is approached on the landward side through a steep wooded valley. The small harbour is typical of those built to provide shelter along the inhospitable, cliff-backed parts of the south-west coast. Stone houses with slate roofs huddle precariously against the hills or cluster on the Cobb, the 1,000-year-old quayside and harbour where fisherman's boats and pleasure craft shelter. The shingle beach, where the Duke of Monmouth landed in 1685 in his attempt to dethrone

*A view of Lyme Regis from near the Cobb, a breakwater built to protect the small ships that shelter in the artificial harbour. Old houses crowd the shore at the Cobb, which inspired scenes in Jane Austen's **Persuasion** and more recently in John Fowles' **The French Lieutenant's Woman**, made into an award-winning film.*

James II, is to the west of the Cobb; to the east lies the small promenade and beach enjoyed by seaside lovers since the eighteenth century, when Lyme was a fashionable watering place, which is no doubt why Jane Austen chose to set an important part of *Persuasion* in the town.

Between Lyme Regis and the mouth of the River Exe at Exmouth lie a number of long-established seaside resorts, including Sidmouth, a sedate town with solid Georgian buildings and an air of respectability derived perhaps from the fact that Queen Victoria stayed here as a young girl. Elizabeth Barrett Browning also stayed here, falling in love with George Hunter, minister of the Nonconformist chapel. To the east of the town are fine cliffs, over which the coast path climbs. Grassy hills to the west lead to Budleigh Salterton which, like other seaside resorts along this coast, is built in a river valley, that of the Otter. Sir John Millais' famous picture of a seaman talking to two boys by the shore, *The Boyhood of Raleigh*, was painted here.

Beyond the River Exe, where the coast makes a long southward sweep, are several resorts distinguished by the red cliffs characteristic of the Devon shoreline. The first of these, Dawlish, is a very Victorian-looking town and has a red sandy beach on which two much-photographed stone stacks known as the Parson and the Clerk have made it familiar to thousands of people. Dawlish was another resort familiar to Jane Austen, who made Elinor Dashwood refer to the town in *Sense and Sensibility*. Teignmouth, also visited by Jane Austen, was favoured by another writer, Fanny Burney, who ventured to bathe in the sea and to describe the event afterwards.

Farther south lies Torquay, the resort referred to by Tennyson as 'the loveliest sea village.' He would hardly say the same today, for the village which was also viewed by Napoleon from the deck of the *Bellerophon* as he waited to be transported to St. Helena is now a large, though still handsome, seaside metropolis spreading over the hillsides which descend steeply to the sea at Oddicombe and Babbacombe Beach, Anstey's Cove, the promontory of Hope's Nose and at Daddyhole. Torquay's harbour on Tor Bay is crowded with pleasure craft of many varieties, while up on the hills behind and along the Royal Terrace

Gardens are entertainments of all kinds. Perhaps it is the nature of its situation, with the hills breaking up the resort into different areas, or it may be the historical evolution of the town, which gives Torquay an atmosphere very different from other resorts of the south coast. Although hopeful promoters, with its mild climate and palm tree-fringed promenade in mind, have named it England's Riviera resort, it is not like the Côte d'Azur either.

At the southern end of Tor Bay lies Brixham, a fishing village which still has lines of trawlers moored in its hill-enclosed harbour, round which the houses and cottages are lined in colourful ranks. Brixham attracts those who like the simple life served up in a sophisticated way, and has good restaurants and entertainment of the subdued kind.

Simplicity and sophistication is also the keynote of Dartmouth, near the mouth of the River Dart, which is perhaps not surprising as the town is the home of the Royal Naval College, which produces most of the officers of the Senior Service and has trained more than one king of England. The town could hardly be better situated, for the river is broad here and there are wooded hills to each side to shelter the sea entrance where Dartmouth Castle, which may still be visited, was built in the fifteenth century to protect the town against Breton ships. Dartmouth was bombed in World War II, but the main street still has a pleasant old-world air, helped by well-restored seventeenth-century houses in which are boutiques and restaurants.

Devon dips to its southernmost part at Start Point and the land westward to Salcombe estuary; rocky cliffs and surging seas surround the promontory, where there is a nature reserve for sea birds. Start Point, with its lighthouse, has always been a landmark for sailors, giving them their first or last view of England.

From Start Point westward to Plymouth Sound the coastline rises in steep, rugged cliffs and dips down to green valleys with sheltered estuaries, whose waters in summer sparkle with the white sails of small yachts. Along the rock-strewn shore are pools where marine life abounds, and tiny coves with sandy beaches reached by little country roads lined with those high-banked hedges which are a feature of the Devon and Cornish countryside.

Thurlestone is a small village on the west side of Devon's most southerly land mass. There is a long beach south of Thurlestone and a very fine stretch of coast to Bolt Head.

Squeezed into its narrow valley, with its houses packed as closely together as the ships in its harbour, Polperro is a picture-postcard fishing port in southern Cornwall. Cars are not allowed in the narrow village streets which, in summer, are crowded with visitors.

Most people probably remember Plymouth, the largest city in the region, for the story of Sir Francis Drake coolly continuing his game of bowls while the Spaniards sailed up the Channel in 1588. Plymouth Hoe, where the game was supposed to have been played, now has little resemblance to the Hoe of Drake's time. The fine stretch of green lawns, with the Royal Naval War Memorial rising at its centre, is a busy place with plenty of other entertainments besides bowling going on, and traffic swirling by in front of the houses that border it. Much of Plymouth was destroyed in World War II, but some of the old port remains to the east of the Hoe at Sutton Harbour, whose entrance is overlooked by a citadel built by Charles II, who was a great supporter of the Navy. By the quayside in the old harbour a stone commemorates the departure of the Pilgrim Fathers for America in the *Mayflower* and *Speedwell* in 1620.

The River Tamar to the west of Plymouth is the frontier between Devon and Cornwall and the railway link across it is made by a fine bridge built by Isambard Kingdom Brunel, one of the most inventive engineers of the nineteenth century. The Tamar is usually busy with naval shipping, as it has been since the days of the Hundred Years War against the French.

Westward, the coast becomes more rugged and the seas more restless as England reaches out into the Atlantic. The south coast of Cornwall, however, is protected from the fiercest weather by the land, which runs towards the southwest, and by the river estuaries, which run deep inland providing shelter for fishermen, yachtsmen and the summer holiday crowds that arrive to enjoy the surf and sunshine. Though popular in summer, this part of England is rarely overcrowded, for there are few main roads and the motorist rarely ventures down the narrow, winding lanes which lead to such delightful and unspoiled villages as Portscatho and Portloe or to the uninhabited headlands protected by the National Trust.

Where there are good expanses of sand and access is relatively easy there are greater concentrations of visitors, especially where the village has the picturesque qualities of West and East Looe. Polperro, where summer visitors must leave their cars outside the village and walk into its narrow little streets, could be said to have turned picturesqueness into a fine art. Mevagissey, a fishing port where shark-fishing boats in the double harbour offer an exciting day out for visitors, and Gorran Haven, at the foot of a steep and wooded valley and with a good beach, are other popular spots.

Carrick Roads, where several west Cornish rivers reach the sea, is flanked by St. Mawes, a pretty resort with a fine wooded estuary where boats lie like a giant fleet at anchor, and Falmouth. This port, founded by Sir Walter Raleigh and one of the busiest in England until the middle of Victoria's reign, became famous in the nineteenth century for the Falmouth packets which raced each other across the Atlantic as they struggled to win mail contracts. Falmouth skippers and crews had a reputation for toughness and ruthlessness, and for skill and daring, despite all of which they lost the mail packet business to the steamships. Above Falmouth harbour entrance stands Pendennis Castle built by Henry VIII.

At the head of Carrick Roads is Truro, a cathedral city with pleasant Georgian buildings along its busy streets. Once a port for the tin industry, it lost its importance owing to the silting up of the Truro River, which connects it to Carrick Roads, but it has remained the most important town in Cornwall.

One of the best ways of appreciating the beauty of the south coast of Cornwall is to take a boat up almost any of its sheltered creeks, where the steep banks are thick with trees and little villages or isolated cottages peep out from the rich vegetation. In the mornings, before the sea mist clears, the effect of gliding silently up these hidden worlds is magical, and it is easy to believe that the stories

Lizard Point is the most southerly peninsula in Britain, and has a score of unspoiled villages along its rugged coast. Cadgwith Cove has a cluster of cottages round a beach where the boats of fishermen who fish for crab and lobster are drawn up.

The abbey that tops St. Michael's Mount, offshore by Marazion in Cornwall, was associated with its French counterpart Mont St. Michel at the time of Edward the Confessor. The castle was built later and is the home of the St. Aubyn family. Access to the island is across a causeway at low tide or by boat.

of King Arthur and his knights that are part of the Cornish legend are indeed true. One of the most beautiful of the creeks is that of the Helford River, off which lies Frenchman's Creek, made famous by Daphne du Maurier; another, farther east, is Fowey Creek, the setting for part of the Tristan and Isolde story.

As one approaches the Lizard, the most southerly point of mainland Britain, the coast becomes uncompromisingly rugged, and above the cliffs the trees give way to heather and gorse and rock-strewn fields hemmed in by stone walls. Along this wave-fretted coast, pounded in winter by the Atlantic rollers, there are many small villages clinging precariously to the sides of ravines or sheltering in tiny coves. At Coverack, the lifeboat station reminds one of the risks that sailors run in these waters; the Manacles, a reef of rocks out to sea, has been the cause of many a shipping tragedy, many of whose victims lie in the graveyard of St. Keverne church, just inland from Porthoustock.

Lizard Point forms one pincer of the Cornish claw of land reaching into the Atlantic, the other being Land's End. Between these two rocky cliff promontories lies Mount's Bay, which faces the Atlantic. Along it are little coves which, like Mullion Cove, are protected by a sea wall across the rocky entrance or, like Prussia Cove, face east and away from the prevailing winds and waves. In the lee of Land's End is the most sheltered part of the bay and here, rising like a fairy castle out of the sea, is St. Michael's Mount. This conical island capped by a castle lies a quarter of a mile (400 m) offshore from Marazion and is the English counterpart of the Mont St. Michel of northern France. Both have a monastery said to have been founded at the command of St. Michael and both are popular tourist attractions. At low tide the journey to St. Michael's Mount can be made on foot across a causeway, but at other times a ferry must be used. Edward the Confessor founded a priory on the Mount, but legend has it that King Arthur and his knights also lived on it when it was part of the long-lost kingdom of Lyonnesse.

Apart from Penzance, a large resort along the flat western sweep of Mount's Bay and tucked into the lee of Land's End, the coast is full of small fishing villages, such as Mousehole which, like Newlyn, is famed as an artists' paradise discovered nearly a hundred years ago by Dame Laura Knight. Porthcurno is another place well worth a visit, and in summer the Greek-style Minack theatre, cut into the cliff, provides one of the most exciting auditoria in the world.

Penzance is the departure place, by boat or helicopter, for the Isles of Scilly, a group of 145 isles and islets about 28 miles (45 km) out to sea off Land's End. Six of the islands, all of which are gorse- and scrub-covered, with only a few trees to soften the outline, are uninhabited. St. Mary's is the largest and has three-quarters of the total population of the whole group, as well as the port and airstrip, both of which are of vital importance to the Scillies' main sources of income: tourism and flower-growing.

Land's End itself is something of a disappointment, with its tourist litter and coachloads of sightseers catered for by uninspired cafés. More impressive is Cape Cornwall, four miles (6 km) to the north, and the only 'cape' in England and Wales, where the seas crash in against a lonely landscape of wind-blown grass and stone walls. Here the coast turns north-east towards the Bristol Channel, and the long sea swells of the Atlantic batter themselves against high, dark cliffs that can best be seen from the coastal paths that follow the cliffs. By car, the cliff edge can be reached at Pendeen Watch, where there is a lighthouse, and Zennor Head. The grey granite at Zennor is well-known and used in local building. In the church here the figure of a mermaid is carved on one of the pews; according to local legend, she enticed away into the sea the young lord of the manor, whose beautiful singing had attracted her. There are some splendid views from the road to St. Ives, which runs along a corniche above the coast here.

On this restless coast, built on an isthmus at the western side of St. Ives Bay, the old fishing port and resort of St. Ives is a model of tranquillity, with its sandy beach and its white houses sitting sedately on the hillside that shelters the bay from the west winds. St. Ives faces east, and its curving bay, edged with firm clean sands, is much sought after by summer visitors. Virginia Woolf was one of these; she wrote part of *To the Lighthouse* at Hayle, a town with a rather dilapidated Victorian atmosphere halfway along the bay. Today, Hayle is a small port for the surviving Cornish tin-mining industry, though catering for holidaymakers is still its main business, at least in summer.

A few miles to the north the coast resumes its spectacular character at aptly named Hell's Mouth, an overhanging clifftop around which wheel and scream countless sea birds in an aerial acrobatic display that dazzles the eyes. Most of the north coast of Devon and Cornwall is staggeringly beautiful. High cliffs above rocky shores and reefs alternate with stretches of sandy beach. The wind-blown clifftops are covered in heather and bracken, and a coastal path winds along them dipping down into little ports and villages and occasionally to large resorts. The long Atlantic swell breaking on these shores provides the kind of waves that surfers like and make swimming an exhilarating and sometimes dangerous pastime.

From Hell's Mouth to Trevose Head the landscape is dotted with tall, ruined towers, relics of the times when tin mining vied with fishing as the major occupation of the Cornish people. St. Agnes is a fine example of a Cornish mining village, with many signs of the early workings made by men in search of copper and tin still visible on the cliffs around this quiet little place.

Perranporth and Newquay are two resorts with sandy beaches along this stretch of coast, both of them popular with surfers and indeed with everyone looking for all the enterainments of well-established holiday resorts. Newquay has six main beaches, all with vast expanses of sand at low tide, fringed with cliffs, and well visited in summer. To the north beyond the sands lie the jagged rocks of the Bedruthan Steps, which can be seen from the clifftop.

Sir Walter Raleigh, who was Warden of Cornwall, had one of his headquarters at Padstow, and the port, on the west bank of the River Camel estuary, still retains many of the buildings of his period as well as some from earlier times. The picturesqueness of the port is enhanced during the May Day celebrations, when the colourful Padstow hobby horse cavorts about the streets accompanied by other revellers.

North of Padstow we enter King Arthur country, and along the coast at Tintagel lie the remains of what most people think of as his castle. A great fortress of rock, topped by the ruined Tintagel Castle, is reached by a narrow bridge, where the spectacle of the sea crashing on to the rocks below is breathtaking. The cave supposed to have been inhabited by Merlin the magician is below the fortress, and visitors with romantic dispositions are not disappointed, for the setting is the very stuff of romance. True or false, the story of King Arthur draws the crowds in large numbers to visit the place and to buy the many and various King Arthur souvenirs on offer.

Tales of magic and witchcraft, perhaps derived from Merlin's proximity, are also the theme at Boscastle, where the witchcraft museum attracts good custom. This pretty little village is typically Cornish; a narrow entrance between rocks allows boats to sail into the narrow harbour at high tide, where they lie on the mud when the tide recedes or are hauled on to the stone quayside among the nets and lobster pots. The village itself is squeezed between the steep slopes of the valley, watered by a small stream. Despite its popularity, Boscastle has an unspoiled air, as there is no traffic other than through the road in the upper village.

Another of those deadly reefs that stand off the coasts of Cornwall, the Strangles, can be viewed from the High Cliff (731 feet/223 m) near Boscastle. A path leads down its grassy slope to the shore. Beyond Cambeak Point to the north lies Crackington Haven, an isolated village overlooking a sandy bay dominated by a 430-foot (131-m) cliff.

At Bude the cliffs are lower in height and there is a long, sandy stretch of beach which is generally crowded with bathers and surfers during the summer.

Above: The Bedruthan Steps, which legend says were stepping stones for a giant, are north of Newquay along a dramatic section of coast which bears the brunt of the Atlantic rollers from the west.

Above right: Boscastle, near Tintagel, is a pretty village carefully preserved from over-development and has a long, narrow harbour with old buildings now used as shops or cafés and a witchcraft museum. Five miles (8 km) away are the impressive cliffs of Crackington Haven.

Right: The legendary King Arthur is supposed to have had his castle at Tintagel, but the present castle was built in the twelfth century by the Earl of Cornwall. Nevertheless, the Arthurian legend persists and enhances the beautiful and romantic scenery of this part of Cornwall.

Opposite: Clovelly is a carefully preserved fishing village built on a steep, wooded combe leading down to a tiny harbour. No cars are allowed into the village, but one can approach the upper Clovelly car park through the woods of Hobby Drive, which overlook the sea.

Beyond, the coast rises sharply again towards the beautiful area around Morwenstow, where the small village and church nestle at the top of a wooded valley leading down to the sea. Many shipwreck victims are buried in the graveyard which slopes down the hill. Along a path that leads to the edge of the 450-foot (137-m) cliff is the hut built by Robert Hawker, the nineteenth-century poet and vicar of Morwenstow. Visitors may still take tea in the vicar's garden.

At Hartland Point, with its sea-dashed slabs of rock, the Atlantic swells meet the waters of the Bristol Channel, creating turbulent water at the changes of the tide. There is a path leading down to the lighthouse, which can be visited during summer. An even more impressive spectacle is to be seen at Hartland Quay to the south, where the jagged rocks and cliffs, rising among a continually surging and breaking sea, look dangerous even on calm days.

This is the mariners' coast which, in Elizabethan times, provided many of the men who manned the ships that sailed the Atlantic and beyond. Many of the ships were built in the quiet estuaries of Bideford and Barnstaple, which lie at the eastern end of Bideford Bay, a particularly charming stretch of coast where small villages cling to the slopes of the cliffs and ravines. The most famous and the most visited of these is Clovelly, which has tea rooms, souvenir shops and restaurants galore in its little white-painted cottages on its steeply sloping cobbled street.

Bideford, on the River Torridge, was once a busy seaport and still receives the occasional coaster to moor alongside the long river front of the town's main street. Bideford was Sir Richard Grenville's departure point for America in the sixteenth century, when the town was one of the largest ports in England, and the 24-arched bridge which spans the river today was built at this time. In the Royal Hotel, at the eastern end of the bridge, Charles Kingsley wrote *Westward Ho!*, a tale of Elizabethan sea adventure.

Barnstaple, spreading extensively on flat land by the River Taw, was another busy Elizabethan seaport and, like Bideford, enjoyed success as a port until the nineteenth century. From here, wool was shipped abroad and the products of the New World were distributed throughout Britain. An attractive part of the town is Queen Anne's Walk, which still has the narrow streets and old buildings of the time when sailors and merchants thronged the bars and coffee shops, and John Gay, author of *The Beggar's Opera*, went to school near the parish church.

The low-lying land around Barnstaple rises to the north to a superb stretch of cliff-dominated coast, extending from Woolacombe in Devon, a vast sandy beach backed by huge sand dunes, to Minehead in Somerset, a popular resort dominated by North Hill, which marks the last high land of the coast. This is the coast of the Exmoor National Park, where the land arrives abruptly at the sea, dropping hundreds of feet to the waves but cut here and there by steep, wooded combes, down which the water from the moor runs in turbulent torrents.

Ilfracombe, at the western end of this coast, is beautifully situated between hills and sea and has at least seven separate beaches. It is such a popular place with holidaymakers that most of its delightfully Victorian houses, standing in serried ranks along the hills, have been turned into hotels and guest houses. As one might expect in a place that has been a port since medieval times, there is much activity on the quaysides, though today the seamen take visitors out on sea and fishing trips and to Lundy Island, which is visible on the horizon 23 miles (37 km) away in the Bristol Channel. Lundy was once a haven for pirates and outlaws, but now has only a tiny population of humans and a much greater one of puffins, seals and other wildlife.

There are few roads to the coast along here, and anyone who wants to enjoy its beauty must take a footpath. The most spectacular of these begins at Lynton and travels westwards to Woody Bay, from where the old stagecoach road along the coast can be followed to Hunters Inn on the main road. Farther east, another lovely walk starts at Porlock Weir and skirts the edge of Porlock Hill, giving fine views of the coast below. Lynton is said to have been made popular by the Romantic poets. Shelley stayed there with his young wife, Harriet, and Wordsworth and Coleridge loved walking in the steep, wooded valleys which retain all the features, including rocks, trees, rushing streams and waterfalls, so loved by the Romantics.

Above: The village of Lynmouth, in north Devon, lines the banks of the River Lyn, which drops through a steep and picturesque ravine to the sea. Above it is Lynton, perched on the side of the steep hill down which a cliff railway operates to the lower resort.

Eastward from Minehead, the waters of the sea begin to lose their blue as the river waters of the Wye and Severn mingle with the Atlantic. The wild character of the coast tones down to an area of green farmlands and woods stretching far inland into the fertile fields of Somerset. Vast areas of sand provide holiday beaches for inhabitants of inland towns and cities. Burnham-on-Sea and Weston-super-Mare are large Victorian resorts with all the amenities of popular resorts. Clevedon, farther north, is smaller and retains a fine Victorian atmosphere, including an attractive pier, now sadly closed and decaying.

Bristol, reached from the sea up the River Avon, is in a sense the capital of the sea-going west. For centuries the ships that have plied the coasts of Devon, Cornwall and Somerset, faced the hazards of long sea voyages and the final beat

up the dangerous western coasts, have been heading for Bristol. John Cabot sailed from here on his voyage of discovery to Newfoundland, and Robert Louis Stevenson summed up the romanticism of the great port of the west in *Treasure Island*. The famous Bristol pub, the Llandoger Trow, was the Spyglass of Stevenson's book. Slavery, wine and port helped to build up many of the most attractive areas of the city one sees today, among the highlights of which are the cathedral, begun in the twelfth century; the old dock area where you will find the Bristol Old Vic theatre; the Clifton Suspension Bridge built by Brunel across the gorge through which the River Avon leaves the city; and Brunel's *Great Britain*, the first ocean screw steamship, which was wrecked in the Falkland Islands and is now being rebuilt in its home dock.

Overleaf: Though some distance from the Bristol Channel, the city of Bristol has been an important port since America was discovered, thanks to the channel provided by the River Avon. The Avon Gorge is crossed by the Clifton Suspension Bridge designed by the ingenious Isambard Kingdom Brunel.

West Country Moors

The moors of the West Country – Dartmoor, Exmoor and Bodmin – are the wildest expanses of country left in southern England and today are used mainly for sheep grazing, with some farming along their fringes or in sheltered valleys. Riders and walkers enjoy the freedom of unfenced roads and the heather- and bracken-covered land where they can roam at will.

The three moors vary in character, with open moor, wooded valleys, rocky summits and little villages contained within a relatively small area of land. They also vary considerably in mood according to the weather; smiling and open on a summer's day or dour and threatening when bad weather closes in, they become mysterious on those days when the mist swirls over the land. Dartmoor is the largest and best-known of the moors, and is associated in the public mind with the prison at Princeton and the fiendish hound of the Baskervilles created by Arthur Conan Doyle. Even today, anyone who has read the story feels a shiver of apprehension on hearing a dog baying across the moor on a misty day.

The most northerly point of the moor is Okehampton, a market town with the remains of a Norman castle. Near here are Dartmoor's highest points, the granite peaks, or tors, of High Willhays (2,039 feet/621 m) and Yes Tor (2,028 feet/618 m). From here, the views to the south on a fine day are particularly splendid. Wild Dartmoor ponies may often be encountered on the lonely moorland near here, where the rivers Taw, Tavy, Dart and Teign begin their journeys to the sea. To the south-east of the moor lies the village celebrated in the Devon song about friends who went to Widecombe Fair only to return on a grey mare that was the devil in disguise; no doubt there had been a drop or two of Devon cider drunk in the local pub. Widecombe is still a small village which, inevitably though discreetly, exploits its fame.

Farther south and inland west of Torbay is Buckfast Abbey, founded by King Canute, though the present large abbey church is a modern building completed in 1938 by the Benedictine monks who live there and whose tonic wines and honey are sold to visitors. The abbey is near Buckfastleigh, a pretty village that is the northern terminus of the privately owned Dart Valley Steam Railway.

Other abbeys in this part of Devon include Buckland, founded in the thirteenth century but turned into a private mansion at the time of the dissolution of the monasteries; it is now a museum and has some relics of Sir Francis Drake, who lived here. Yet another important Benedictine abbey stood at Tavistock to the north, but only a few ruins remain today. Tavistock itself, a market town, is largely Victorian in character.

Exmoor, lying to the north, falls mostly within the county boundaries of Somerset. It is much smaller and less rugged than Dartmoor, though it can offer the true, bare wind-blown atmosphere of moors, especially at such places as Dunkery Beacon, its highest point (1,706 feet/520 m), from where there are fine views across the Bristol Channel to the mountains of Wales. The name most associated with Exmoor is Lorna Doone, the heroine of R. D. Blackmore's novel. Blackmore lived in Devon and was educated at Tiverton. The Doone valley, where Lorna's robber family lived, is a popular tourist spot, though quite unspoiled, and can only be reached on foot from the little village of Brendon.

Over the hill to the south of the Doone valley is the River Exe, which flows south to Exeter and Exmouth. Its very pretty valley runs parallel to that of the Barle, on which lies the attractive wooded village of Simonsbath, a good fishing centre. Farther south along the valley are the mysterious Tarr Steps, a primitive stone bridge whose origin and builders are unknown.

Among the many attractive villages in the Exmoor area is Dunster, in a particularly interesting valley at the eastern end of the moor. The medieval Yarn Market dominates the High Street, which is lined with old stone houses; there is an inhabited castle which can be visited, and the church boasts the widest choir-screen of any parish church in England.

Bodmin Moor in Cornwall is even smaller than Exmoor but is a much wilder and more desolate place. The town of Bodmin, at the south-western edge of the moor, is the county town of Cornwall. From Bodmin the road runs across the moor to Launceston, near the Devon border, passing Bolventor on the way. The

Jamaica Inn of this cluster of houses was used as the title of Daphne du Maurier's novel about smugglers. Also close to Bolventor is Dozmary Pool where, according to legend, King Arthur's sword Excalibur was cast into the waters. The highest point of Bodmin Moor, Brown Willy (1,375 feet/419 m), can be seen from the road to Bolventor. As with the other moors, the best parts of Bodmin Moor can only be enjoyed on horseback or on foot.

Above: Exmoor stretches across north Devon and into Somerset. This was once a royal hunting ground and is still the home of the red deer. The Doone valley is the setting of R. D. Blackmore's novel about Lorna Doone, and at Dunster there is a fine castle and old town.

Around the Mendip Hills

The Mendip Hills rise between the plain of the River Parrett in Somerset and the Cotswolds and, though small in area and low of height, have a character of their own. Like most western hill country, they have temperamental weather caused by their position as bastions against the clouds borne by the prevailing south-west winds. Their scenery is as varied as the weather. In the south-east the hills rise gently, at their centre are moorlands, and at their north-west edge the hills are cut by gorges, of which the Cheddar Gorge is the most famous.

Cheddar village is at the entrance to the famous limestone gorge where Ice Age people lived and which today, in high summer, becomes crowded with visitors bent on exploring the mysteries of the caverns. To the south-east along the line of hills is another natural wonder, Wookey Hole. The River Axe flows through these limestone caves, three of which are floodlit for better viewing. One of the best-known features in the caves is the stalagmite called the 'Witch of Wookey', a natural effigy of a witch who, legend has it, lived in the caves.

A few miles to the south-west of Wookey is one of England's finest cathedrals, surrounded by a charming old town. Wells Cathedral has a superb west front, with more embellishments and statues than are usually found on English cathedrals. The interior can also show unusual features, including inverted arches and a charming collection of carved pillars depicting everyday life during the twelfth to fourteenth centuries when the cathedral was being built. Still farther to the south-east is the delightful village of Shepton Mallet, an important wool town in medieval times, with an interesting church and a market place with the remains of its fifteenth-century meat market, or Shambles, still to be seen. From Shepton

Right: The impressive Cheddar Gorge is a two-mile-long (3-km) canyon in the Mendip Hills. The limestone is perforated with caves, in which have been found Stone Age tools and weapons and the skeleton of an Ice Age man. South-east along the Mendips is Wookey Hole, a series of caverns through which runs the River Axe.

Preceding page: The thatch-roofed stone cottages of Buckland-in-the-Moor, at the south-east corner of Dartmoor, are a great attraction to visitors to this part of Devon. Along the road to the north lies Widecombe in the Moor, whose fair inspired the famous Devon song.

Mallet to the east and south-east lie two great English houses, Longleat House near Frome and Montacute on a tributary of the River Parrett.

To the south-west of the Mendips the land is green and fertile, with a few rounded hills rising from the plain. Among these is Glastonbury Tor, which dominates the charismatic little town of Glastonbury, once the home of one of England's greatest abbeys. The ruins that remain on grassy slopes in the town give some idea of the vastness of Glastonbury Abbey; even the kitchen is on a large scale, evoking the pleasures of the table for which the monks were renowned. The legend of Glastonbury tells of the arrival of Joseph of Arimathea in that part of England to preach Christianity and of his wooden staff taking root where he pressed it into the ground. A thorn tree in the abbey grounds today is said to have come from the original thorn that sprouted from the saint's staff.

Overleaf: Bradford-on-Avon is an attractive town which echoes the style of nearby Bath to the north. Its church of St. Laurence dates back to the eighth and tenth centuries, but most of the stone buildings are seventeenth and eighteenth century.

Bath was known to the Romans, who built lavish baths supplied with waters by thermal springs, but its fame rests on its Georgian architecture. Its crescents, squares, and streets demonstrate the art of elegant city planning, and the fifteenth-century abbey an earlier English flair for church architecture.

Another legend claims that Glastonbury was Avalon, the place to which King Arthur was taken after his death, and that the Holy Grail for which his knights searched is buried under Glastonbury Tor. True or false, there is not doubt that Glastonbury is a place with a magical atmosphere.

To the north the Mendips descend towards the lovely valley of the Avon; in the wooded hills and valleys there are lovely old villages like Mells and Hinton Charterhouse, old inns and famous manor houses like Combe Hay and Welton Manor. The jewel of the Avon is, of course, Bath, once a fashionable spa and still one of the most elegant towns in Britain, despite what many see as crass modern development. The Roman Baths in Bath attest to the high regard in which the Romans held this part of the Avon valley, and the terraced Georgian houses, disposed in squares and wonderfully elegant crescents, show that Bath was the centre of the eighteenth- and early nineteenth-century world of fashion and culture. Fielding, Smollett, Jane Austen and Dickens used Bath as a setting for events in their books, though Sam Weller, the outspoken friend of Mr. Pickwick, did not think much of the water. In addition to its Georgian splendours, largely the work of the architect John Wood, Bath has a fine fifteenth-century abbey and an enchanting riverside on which, at Claverton, lies a Georgian manor house where a fascinating museum of American life has been established.

The Heart of England

Many people look on the Midland counties of England as something of an industrial desert with no history of interest earlier than the nineteenth century. They forget that until the Industrial Revolution, this inland country was rich farmland fought over by medieval barons and settled into by their descendants, the landed gentry of the seventeenth and eighteenth centuries. In fact, there is still more country than town in this historic part of England, fringed by the Chilterns and Cotswolds to the south, the Severn valley to the west, Sherwood Forest to the north-east and the Derbyshire Peak District to the north. This fertile area, dotted with famous castles and fine manor houses, is well watered by rivers. The Trent, rising in the Peak District, makes a great sweep southward through Staffordshire, Derbyshire and Nottingham before joining the Humber; the Welland flows eastward to the Wash; and the Avon, by whose banks Shakespeare walked and meditated, flows west into the valley of the River Severn.

Centres of Power

The Midland counties of England are starred with towns whose names remind one of famous people in Britain's history. The Earl of Warwick, 'the king-maker', was the power behind the throne during the Wars of the Roses, the Earl of Leicester was Elizabeth I's favourite, and the Earl of Derby gave his name to a famous horserace. Other cities became famous the world over in a later age through their industrial might. Birmingham, a centre of iron work in Tudor

The pride of the Peak District of Derbyshire is Chatsworth House, with its superb gardens and park. The present Palladian mansion was built by the Duke of Devonshire between 1687 and 1706, but there was a previous mansion often visited by Mary Queen of Scots when she was a prisoner in the custody of the Earl of Shrewsbury.

The Leycester Hospital, in Warwick, is one of the many medieval buildings in this old county town. The buildings have been occupied for 400 years by retired soldiers known as 'Brethren'. Adjoining the hospital is the town wall and the chapel of St. James.

times when armour for Elizabeth's soldiers was made there, later became the world leader in bicycles, motor cycles and other vehicles. From Stafford came – and still come – famous makes of china, such as Minton, Spode and Wedgwood. At Nottingham, Arkwright introduced steam power into his spinning mills, and the city became known for its lace. North of the city, in Sherwood Forest, lived the legendary outlaw Robin Hood.

Today the centres of many of these cities are being rebuilt, with modern shopping and business centres replacing old street patterns, but much remains to interest historians, amateur or professional, and those who are fascinated by the archaeology of industry.

Birmingham lies at the heart of the Midlands, though nearby Meriden claims to be the very centre of England. The great city, the second largest in Britain, has been extensively rebuilt, much of the shoddiness inevitable in cities built quickly and without care in the nineteenth-century industrial expansion disappearing before the bulldozer. Birmingham has become cosmopolitan too, a process accelerated by the arrival of large numbers of Commonwealth and European workers employed by the new industries that have grown up in place of the old.

Birmingham is surrounded by much beautiful countryside, where canals and rivers water the rich, red soil. Henley-in-Arden, beside the River Alne, rests in the remains of the Forest of Arden, the setting for Shakespeare's *As You Like It*. Coleshill, to the east, is another pretty country village, which has relics of the bad old days when miscreants were put in the stocks or publicly whipped. Maxstoke Castle, a couple of miles away, is a fourteenth-century moated sandstone mansion whose furnishings include the chair on which Henry VII sat to be crowned after the battle of Bosworth. It is just one of many great houses in the country around

Birmingham. Tudor Packwood House is near Hockley Heath to the south-east; Arbury Hall, built on the ruins of an old priory and the birthplace of George Eliot, the novelist, is to the north-east; Hagley Hall, home of the Lytteltons since the thirteenth century (though the house is much more recent), rests in its lovely park a few miles west; and Ragley Hall, home of the Marquesses of Hertford, with gardens landscaped by Capability Brown, lies to the south at Alcester, an attractive old town with timbered houses on the rivers Alne and Arrow.

To the north of Birmingham is Lichfield, a cathedral city destroyed by Cromwell but in which the triple-spired cathedral survived. Dr. Samuel Johnson was born here, and his house is now a museum. East of Birmingham lies Coventry, capital of the car industry and renowned as the city with the great modern cathedral designed by Sir Basil Spence, which was built alongside the ruins of the one destroyed during the devastation of the city by bombing in 1940. The city's more traditional fame rests on Lady Godiva who, in protest at her husband Leofric's cruelty to the townsfolk, rode through the streets naked.

Near Coventry, to the south-west, lies Kenilworth Castle, the setting for one of Sir Walter Scott's best-known novels. To the south are Royal Leamington Spa, a most attractive town rich in Georgian houses, and Warwick, whose great castle, once the fortress of the Beauchamps, Earls of Warwick, and now owned by Madame Tussaud's, looms over the River Avon. Robert Dudley, Earl of Leicester, entertained Elizabeth I in the castle and is buried at St. Mary's Church in the town.

Robert Dudley, Earl of Leicester and favourite of Queen Elizabeth I, was given Kenilworth Castle, formerly owned by John of Gaunt, by the queen. Cromwell's soldiers later destroyed it, but the restoration of the ruins has recreated this great stronghold.

Above: Braunston, west of Northampton, is an important inland waterway junction and starting point for cruises along the Grand Union Canal. It was created in 1929 by joining the Grand Junction Canal, which runs from the Thames, and the Oxford and the Midland Canals.

Left: This strange triangular lodge was built by Sir Thomas Tresham, a devout Roman Catholic, in the grounds of Rushton Hall, near Kettering. Dating from 1593, it is full of religious significance, its three sides, three floors, three-sided chimney stack and trefoil windows all symbolizing the Holy Trinity. According to legend, this was one of the meeting places of Guy Fawkes and his fellow conspirators.

Another of the five industrial cities clustered in England's centre is Northampton on the River Nene, which flows out past Peterborough to the Wash. The main industry in Northampton is the making of footwear, the leather for which was once tanned with the bark of trees that grew in the valley. Though a busy town, Northampton escapes the grime and squalor one usually associates with industry. There is some beautiful countryside at hand along the Nene valley, on whose slopes to the east lies Castle Ashby, where the Marquesses of Northampton live amid beautiful grounds landscaped by Capability Brown.

A short drive out of Northampton on the Rugby Road brings one to Althorp, seat of the Earls Spencer, and famous both for its superb collection of pictures, which includes works by Van Dyck, Lely, Kneller, Gainsborough and Reynolds, and for the fact that one of the daughters of the Spencer family, Diana, is now Princess of Wales. To the north-east, roads lead into a particularly attractive part of the Northamptonshire countryside, where woodlands that were once part of great forests survive amid the green fields. In Rockingham Forest lies Fotheringhay, a pretty village by the River Nene where once stood the castle in which the ill-fated Mary Queen of Scots was beheaded.

Fotheringhay lies at the eastern end of Leicestershire, in whose centre is its county town, Leicester, which thrives on footwear and hosiery although, being in the centre of a rich farming area, it also has the air of a market town. Its New Walk, flanked by trees, lawns and Victorian houses, is an attractive area close to the busy new business centre. Evidence that this was once a Roman town remains near the Jewry Wall, and an example of medieval Leicester can be seen at the timbered Guildhall.

All around here is great hunting country, and the names of Melton Mowbray and Belvoir are familiar to everyone interested in the sport of fox-hunting. The village of Belvoir is dominated by its castle, a Gothic-style early nineteenth-century replacement for the previous one, which was largely destroyed by fire in 1816. The castle dominates the lovely Vale of Belvoir and its owner, the Duke of Rutland, is at present fighting as doughty a fight as any of his ancestors, this time against the Coal Board who want to mine the vale for the rich seams of coal which lie beneath it.

To the west of the Midlands, in Staffordshire, lies the industrial area once called the Black Country because of its industrial griminess. Modern methods

Overleaf: The River Dove has worn a ravine through the hills of the southern Peak District creating a lovely wooded gorge called Dove Dale.

Left: Among the many splendid half-timbered houses of Cheshire is Little Moreton Hall. This Elizabethan manor house lies near Congleton, north of the Pottery Towns.

Below: Near Leek, which lies on the western edge of the Peak District, is a range of hills called the Roaches. Among these, Hen Cloud stands out as a rugged mass of millstone grit above the surrounding fields.

have changed all that, though the industry remains. At Stoke-on-Trent, the centre of the Potteries district, which has absorbed the five towns made famous in Arnold Bennett's novels, still has a busy life turning out china, much of it for export. Even in Stoke the country is not far away. Alton Towers, the show garden made by a nineteenth-century Earl of Shrewsbury out of wild hill land, is still a marvellous place and now includes model railways, lakes, and Italian-style buildings among its attractions, as well as the Towers, a great nineteenth-century mansion. Hawksmore Nature Reserve, owned by the National Trust, is also close by.

Stafford, the county town, is a charming place on the River Sow and has managed to preserve some of the buildings in streets that still trace the medieval shape of the town. High House, which once provided shelter for Charles I, and Tudor Swan Hotel date back to Tudor times. The river curves round the town, and no doubt young Izaak Walton, who was born here, spent many hours fishing off its banks. To the south-east lies Cannock Chase, once a royal forest and now a vast area where the public can enjoy the countryside.

Wolverhampton, which was the capital of the Black Country, remains industrial with considerable iron and steel works, but the replanning and

rebuilding of the town has turned it from an industrial horror into an acceptable industrial city. Rural scenery is not far away along the banks of the Staffs and Worcester Canal. Wightwick House, though nineteenth century, is worth a visit, if only for its original William Morris materials. Moseley Old Hall, to the north, is an Elizabethan house where Charles II hid after the battle of Worcester.

Though this is the heart of the Black Country, with other industrial towns like Dudley and West Bromwich nearby, there is a surprising amount of green countryside to be enjoyed, but then the whole of the Midlands is surprising in its variety, which ranges from the mountains of the High Peak to the rolling farmland of Leicestershire and makes it an area that demands to be better known.

The Peak District

Northern Derbyshire almost overlooks Greater Manchester, but nothing could be in greater contrast to this vast, sprawling conurbation than the rocky crags and moorlands of the Peak District. Among these hills one can find total isolation, either on the heath-covered moors or grassy slopes of the hills or deep down in the caves, which are a pot-holer's paradise.

Castleton is an attractive village in the midst of the High Peak; above it rise the ruins of Peveril Castle, setting of Sir Walter Scott's novel *Peveril of the Peak*. There is an underground cave under the hill on which the castle stands and many more up the Hope Valley, some of them accessible only by boat. But thrills are not only found underground in this exciting area of the Midlands. The land is ideal for walking and sports of all kinds, including hang-gliding, sailing, rock climbing and gliding. Edale is a centre for outdoor activities of this kind, and from here begins the walk along the Pennine Way to the Scottish border along the high ridge of the Pennine Hills.

In contrast to the austere beauty of the High Peak, where green slopes and stony summits rise above the valley farms, the landscape in southern Derbyshire is gentler and more in miniature. The valleys are called dales here, and the rivers that run through them twist and turn through little gorges, often heavily wooded, or between long smooth slopes covered in grass or stony screes.

Dove Dale is probably the best known and possibly the most beautiful of the dales, which have often been compared to the valleys found in Switzerland. The only way to enjoy Dove Dale's two-mile (3-km) stretch is on foot along the path that follows the river. Another delightful dale is the one in which Matlock is situated. The pretty village is strung along the gorge of the River Derwent and is overlooked by a 750-foot (229-m) ridge of hills, known as the Heights of Abraham because of their similarity to the cliffs which General Wolfe captured at Quebec. Another summit among the high land around here is High Tor which is 380 feet (116 m) above the dale.

Two great houses, both connected with famous ladies, lie to the north of the dales of Matlock. One is Chatsworth, originally a mansion belonging to the Cavendish family. Bess of Hardwick, the wife of Sir William Cavendish, completed the house, which was visited many times by Mary Queen of Scots while she was in the custody of the Earl of Shrewsbury, Bess's fourth husband. The present house was built by the first Duke of Devonshire, Bess's great-great-great-grandson. The house is superbly furnished and contains many works of art. Parts of the gardens were designed by Joseph Paxton, the creator of the Crystal Palace. This was the centrepiece of the Great Exhibition of 1851, which opened people's eyes to the wonders of the industrial age. The other house, equally delightful but older, is Haddon Hall, which is associated with Anne Vernon, wife of Sir John Manners who, legend has it, eloped with him down the steps that lead to the gardens.

Buxton, once a fashionable spa, is the only town of any size in the Peak District. Like Bath, though on a lesser scale, it has some fine Georgian buildings and a crescent opposite the hot springs which eighteenth-century visitors thought they found so beneficial. Today, Buxton is having something of a revival as a centre for visitors to the Peak District and still caters for those who wish to take or to bathe in the waters.

Above: Though damaged by fire in 1969, Anne Hathaway's cottage at Shottery has been restored to look just as it did in Shakespeare's day. The interior contains original furniture, including an Elizabethan bed.

Left: Stratford-upon-Avon is a busier place than in Shakespeare's day, but much of its old atmosphere has been preserved. The tomb of the greatest English dramatist is at Holy Trinity Church by the River Avon.

Preceding pages: Bakewell is a pretty Derbyshire town on the River Wye, which flows down from the High Peak. The bridge over the river dates back to the fourteenth century. The town has given its name to a type of pastry known as Bakewell tart, and is also noted for its well-dressing festival each summer.

Shakespeare Country

Though it receives more tourists than any town in England and the shops, hotels and restaurants are devoted to catering for visitors eager for Shakespeariana, Stratford-upon-Avon, a pleasant town on the River Avon which still holds the weekly market it was granted under royal charter in 1196, manages to cope with its temporary guests with discretion and charm.

Everything in Stratford-upon-Avon that can be associated with Shakespeare is a sight to see for the determined visitor. The half-timbered Tudor house where he was born in Henley Street, the school he attended, the house in which his daughter Susanna lived, the church in which he was buried, the cottage at Shottery associated with his wife, Anne Hathaway, and his mother's birthplace at Wilmcote are all magnets for visitors. Even without Shakespeare, Stratford would be a very attractive town to visit, with its timbered and Georgian houses and gardens, many of them along the river's edge, where the church of the Holy Trinity, containing the bard's grave, and the modern Royal Shakespeare Theatre are also to be found. Administering Stratford-upon-Avon's five most important Shakespeare sites is the Shakespeare Birthplace Trust, whose own modern centre in Henley Street, near the birthplace, is itself a calling place for tourists.

In the peaceful countryside surrounding Stratford are several impressive old houses. Compton Wynyates, considered to be the best example of a Tudor mansion in existence today, lies south-east of Stratford near Shipston-on-Stour. This brick and stone house, with characteristic Tudor chimneys and set in a beautiful garden, lies in lovely countryside so peaceful it seems difficult to believe that the first battle of the Civil War was fought just to the north at Edge Hill. Wynyates was taken by Cromwell, though later returned to its Royalist owners. At Edge Hill itself is another lovely mansion, Upton House, which dates back to the time of William and Mary and has a fine collection of paintings, including some by that English master of the equine scene, George Stubbs. Yet another house cared for by the National Trust is Farnborough Hall, an Italian-style palazzo with views of Edge Hill.

The Wye and Severn Valleys

At its western edge, the heart of England abuts with Wales, and in medieval times the country was a battleground in which border raids were frequent, so it was natural that the lords of the Marches (the border districts) should give a great deal of attention to the building of castles and fortifications. Nowhere is this more apparent than in the lower reaches of the River Wye, which is the frontier between Wales and England from the point at which it enters the Severn, at Chepstow, downriver to Monmouth.

The powerful Norman castle of Chepstow, on the Welsh bank, looks down menacingly over the river from its cliff on one side and over the town with its narrow streets on the other. In the steep-sided wooded valley which it guards lies Tintern Abbey, inspiration of a famous Wordsworth poem and still impressive in its ruined state. The abbey, founded in 1131, was one of the victims of Henry VIII's campaign to curtail the power of the Church and its monasteries.

A main road follows the river closely on the Welsh bank, while on the English side there are fields and what remains of the Forest of Dean. Where the Welsh Monnow joins the Wye at Monmouth there is another castle, this one the birthplace of Henry V. There is not much of it left now except parts of the ward and the great hall. There are numerous attractive Georgian houses in the town and the only fortified bridge left in Britain crosses the Monnow.

Beyond Welsh Monmouth the Wye runs through the English counties of Gloucester, Hereford and Worcester, which push inwards into Wales, and the natural frontier made by the Black Mountains, which loom up to the west. This is generally agreed to be the most beautiful part of the river, with Symonds Yat, where the river flows through a narrow gorge, the high point. The centre of its looping course here is Huntsham Hill, a steep wooded promontory above the green countryside. Goodrich Castle, farther upstream, stands on another commanding hill, its four towers providing excellent viewpoints for spying on enemies or, today, for enjoying the breathtaking views. The castle, once the home of the Earls of Shrewsbury, was destroyed by Cromwell, though some spectacular ruins remain.

The Wye valley forms the border between England and Wales in the lower part of its course, where Tintern Abbey stands. The beautiful abbey, which inspired Wordsworth to write a poem about it, was begun in the eleventh century, but its present form dates back to the thirteenth.

Ross-on-Wye, upstream to the north, is the star town of the Wye valley. Set on a hill above the broad river valley, it has some fine streets of elegant Georgian houses and a seventeenth-century covered market. In addition to its natural charm, Ross-on-Wye is well situated for trips into the Brecon Beacons, Black Mountains and the Wye valley itself.

Hereford, a cathedral city dating back to Saxon times, lies farther north again. The twelfth-century cathedral is the high spot of a visit to this busy market town; among its treasures are a map of the world in the fourteenth century and a chained library which is among the biggest in the world.

Beyond Hereford the Wye's course changes to a west–east line, its swift-running waters flowing off the Welsh mountains where its source lies. On the Welsh side of the border the river runs through Hay-on-Wye, a village known to people interested in books the world over, for here, in the lee of the Black Mountains, is the largest number of second-hand and antiquarian bookshops of

Along the Welsh border below the splendid countryside of the Black Mountains, the River Monnow flows past the Clodock Mills, near Longtown, and down to Monmouth, one of the border towns defended by a powerful castle.

any village in the world. Summer and winter those who like browsing among old books and charming surroundings are attracted here in their thousands.

The River Severn follows a similar, though longer, course to that of the Wye, but it runs farther to the east. Its character is very different, however, at least in its English course. In the lower reaches, as it flows through the Vale of Gloucester before passing under the graceful new suspension bridge, the Severn is a wide, gently moving river bordered by farmland. The cathedral city of Gloucester was founded at its most southerly crossing point, a place that the Romans guarded alertly, building a fort on the river banks. This fort existed into medieval times and the buildings around it, of which some still exist, increased in number. Gloucester cathedral was built over several centuries, its vast Perpendicular-style east window being installed in the fourteenth century to celebrate the victory of Edward III over the French at Crècy. The lovely fan-vaulted cloisters also date from the same century.

The junction of the River Avon and the Severn was another important crossing point, and here the town of Tewkesbury grew. The Normans built an abbey church here – one of the most splendid in England – and its 100-foot (30-m) tower is now part of the Church of St. Mary the Virgin. According to legend, the abbey was saved from Henry VIII's destructive campaign by the people of the town, who bought the building from him. With its half-timbered houses and narrow streets Tewkesbury has preserved strong links with its past, which include the part it played in the Wars of the Roses when the Yorkist claimant to the throne, Edward IV, won a decisive battle against the Lancastrians here.

Between Tewkesbury and Shrewsbury, where the river begins to turn southwards, there is some lovely countryside with views of the Welsh mountains to the west. Closer to the river, north-west of Tewkesbury, are the Malvern Hills, a popular area in the days of the spas and still well patronized by those who enjoy the country life and splendid walks in the vicinity.

Worcester, whose wonderful cathedral is set in grounds edged by a riverside terrace, is another Severn town with a rich and colourful past. The cathedral itself was founded in 983 by St. Oswald, and the present 750-year-old building contains the tombs of King John and of Arthur, son of Henry VII. All that now remains of the monastery that was also once a feature of medieval Worcester is the Edgar Tower, the cloisters and a refectory which is now part of King's school. During the Civil War, Worcester was a Royalist town and was the scene of Charles II's defeat by Cromwell in 1651. The house in New Street in which he

narrowly escaped capture is a fine half-timbered building known as King Charles' House. Both Charles and his father, Charles I, are commemorated by statues at the Guildhall; the town showed what it thought of Cromwell by pinning an effigy of him by his ears to a doorway. Worcester has been the home of Worcester porcelain since the mid-eighteenth century, and visits to the factory, which has been on its present site since 1840, are welcome.

Near Worcester the Severn is joined by the River Teme, whose tributary the Corve flows off Wenlock Edge to meet it at Ludlow, whose formidable castle was built to resist Welsh attacks. The two young princes who died in the Tower of London were kept here before being taken to the capital.

North of Worcester, the Severn has the Wyre Forest, the very pretty village of Bewdley on its west bank and, beyond Bridgnorth, the famous Wenlock Edge hills which inspired some of the lines of A. E. Housman's *A Shropshire Lad*. Upstream from here, the character of the river valley changes as the world of industry intrudes on the rural tranquillity. The Iron Bridge Gorge, through

Ironbridge, on the River Severn north of the town of Bridgnorth was one of the centres where the Industrial Revolution began. A symbol of those significant days is the first iron bridge ever to be built, which dates from 1799 and is still used for pedestrian traffic.

This handsome half-timbered building in Shrewsbury was the Gateway to the Council House in which Charles I had his headquarters in 1642. The Gateway stands near the castle, which has been rebuilt twice since it was founded in the eleventh century, once by Edward I and the second time by Thomas Telford in the nineteenth century.

which the river passes, was involved in the very beginnings of the Industrial Revolution and the iron bridge itself, an imposing structure some 200 feet (61 m) long at Ironbridge, was a harbinger of things to come.

Shrewsbury, which lies near the Welsh border, where the river that tumbles off the Welsh mountains begins to acquire its English character, is a memorable town round which the river runs in a great loop. In many parts of the town one can be easily transported back to Tudor times by the abundance of half-timbered buildings; this is especially so in Grope Lane where the architecture has not changed much since the days of Elizabeth I. Among other earlier buildings in the town are St. Mary's Church (twelfth century) and the Norman castle, which was rebuilt in the fourteenth century. Though on the whole a traditional place, Shrewsbury was the birthplace of two very controversial figures in British history, Clive of India and Charles Darwin.

The source of the Severn lies to the west in the same range of mountains, the Plynlimon, from which springs the Wye.

The North of England

The Mersey, flowing west, and the Humber, flowing east, mark the dividing line between the Midlands and the North of England. Both rivers rise in the Pennines, a range of mountains that extend from the Peak District of Derbyshire up to the Scottish border and which separate the north-eastern from the north-western counties. This geographical splitting of the country has had a significant influence on the development of northern culture, creating an age-old rivalry between the people of Yorkshire and Lancashire, which still comes to the fore in a more – though, some would say, not much more – amicable way at cricket matches and other sporting events, where it sometimes seems as if the Wars of the Roses are being re-enacted.

The Industrial Revolution brought in a mutuality of purpose to both sides of the Pennines, though even then there were differences in the industries that developed. Lancashire, because of its proximity to Liverpool, where raw materials from overseas docked, developed a vast cotton industry while Yorkshire created a woollen industry from the yarn of the sheep sheared on the slopes of the Pennines and the Yorkshire Wolds. The coal and iron common to both counties created great industries which ranged from the mining of the ore to chemicals and heavy engineering. Towns such as Huddersfield, Halifax, Leeds, Burnley and Bradford grew prodigiously while Manchester, joined to Liverpool by the Manchester Ship Canal, became not only a manufacturing centre but the clearing house for local industry.

Swaledale, with its deep valley, in which the River Swale runs from the high Pennines to the north Yorkshire plain, is one of the most beautiful Yorkshire dales. Stone farmhouses are the rule in the hills, where sheep provide the raw material for the Yorkshire textile industry.

Today the land across the counties of Greater Manchester and the southern parts of Lancashire and Yorkshire is heavily industrialized though it is not entirely devoid of beautiful countryside nearby, especially in the areas near the Pennines, in the fell country of Lancashire and to the east on the Yorkshire Wolds. The coasts of both counties provide people from the inland industrial conurbations with places to escape to in summertime, so it is not surprising that some of England's largest seaside resorts are to be found here.

The Coasts of Lancashire and Yorkshire

The traveller interested in the character of the people among whom he travels will find the shores of Lancashire and Yorkshire of special interest, for the resorts along them were created specifically to satisfy the needs of those who work in the large industrial hinterland. The word 'cosmopolitan', sometimes applied to southern resorts, is out of place here, as is 'glamorous'. Neither is missed, for the northern resorts are geared to provide everything that their patrons desire. The beaches are good, and some of the best in England; the entertainments are abundant, both indoors and out, day and night, and include entertainers of international standing. In true northern fashion, the food is plentiful and satisfying.

On the western, Lancashire coast, the seaside begins at the Wirral, the long peninsula extending out of Cheshire between the Dee and the Mersey. The Dee, though much silted up since the days when Nelson sailed up it and stayed with Emma Hamilton at Parkgate, is still a much sought-after area both as a commuter district for Liverpool workers and as a holiday coast, and the views of the Welsh mountains across the river are magnificent, as the painter Turner found.

Inland on the Dee and at the gateway to the lovely Cheshire contryside is Chester. Much of the Roman wall around the city remains, and it encloses one of the finest collections of timbered buildings in Britain, including the Rows, where the buildings overhang balustraded walkways. Chester Cathedral is fourteenth-century.

Merseyside itself has no pretensions to seaside. Birkenhead is a busy industrial and port area and so is Liverpool, one of Britain's most important ports, whose

Above left: The half-timbered houses of Chester, with their overhung first-floor galleries, are unique in Britain. The cathedral city was once a Roman fort, whose walls can still be traced under part of the medieval walls that surround the city today.

famous buildings include two cathedrals, a porticoed St. George's Hall and the Walker Art Gallery. Liverpool extends along the entire eastern side of the Mersey from Widnes to Crosby, where the river empties into the Irish Sea.

North of Formby, edged with sand dunes, lies Southport, an elegant town built in the eighteenth century which has carefully preserved its dignity on a coast where the general tendency is to throw gentility to the winds and let enjoyment reign unconfined. The main shopping area, Lord Street, is one of the most attractive in England and Hesketh Park the finest open space of any Lancashire resort. In contrast, Blackpool, farther up the coast past the Ribble estuary, is a jovial, fun-loving, colourful place, which attempts to keep a party atmosphere going throughout the summer and well into the autumn too. The highspot weeks of the summer are when the factories and industries in the inland towns close down and release thousands of their workers to enjoy themselves. By

St. George's Hall, Liverpool, dominates Lime Street. Its Greek temple style was designed by Harvey Lonsdale Elmes in 1839. In the interior are assize courts and a concert room. To the north of the hall is the 115-foot (35-m) Wellington Column.

131

the end of the season, some eight million people have visited Blackpool each year.

There are six miles (10 km) of sea-front promenade, lit up brightly in the autumn when the Blackpool Illuminations are switched on; there are fun fairs and bingo parlours and, as a reminder of things past, a 518-foot (158-m) tower made of iron girders like the Eiffel Tower and a tramway transport system.

Lancashire's county town, Lancaster, lies to the north of Blackpool. Reminders of the powerful John of Gaunt, Duke of Lancaster, whose famous lines in Shakespeare's *Richard II*, 'this precious stone set in a silver sea . . . this earth, this realm, this England' are perhaps the most moving patriotic speech ever made, are strong in Lancaster. Gaunt enlarged the Norman castle, leaving an impressive memorial of his own power and that of the throne which his son occupied as Henry IV. The town is on the River Lune and the old Customs House is a reminder of its importance as a port in the Middle Ages.

Urban development links the county town to the resorts of Heysham and Morecambe, both doing their best to rival Blackpool. From here there are fine views across Morecambe Bay, famous for its sunsets, to the mountains of the Lake District, an easily assessible and wonderful territory for excursions by visitors to the seaside.

Across the Irish Sea to the west is the Isle of Man, a popular holiday island whose fishing ports produce the famous Manx kippers. The western side of the island is rugged, with attractive cliff-enclosed harbours like Port Erin, Port St. Mary and Peel, while the north-eastern end of the island has superb beaches backed by soft, green countryside. Douglas, the capital and the biggest and liveliest resort, and Ramsey, with its half-mile-long (800-m) pier, are situated here.

Across the Pennines, the North Sea coast is just as much a playground for the dwellers in the industrial cities as is the Lancashire coast. In many parts, however, the coast is a little more hilly, with lines of low cliffs lining the shore. In the far north, in the county of Tyne and Wear, the coast is heavily industrial from Tynemouth, downriver from Newcastle-upon-Tyne, to Sunderland. This is the industrial heart of north-eastern England, a land of iron, coal and shipbuilding which has suffered in recent years from economic recession and foreign competition. The pressure of these circumstances has encouraged the development of new industries in the region and the rebuilding of some of the factory areas. Newcastle itself, unlike many industrial towns, is worthy of preservation, for its centre has some fine, solid Victorian buildings that rank among the best town architecture of their period. Almost lost among the industrial wastes of the Tyne's southern shore near South Shields is the Saxon church of St. Paul's, part of the monastery of Jarrow where in the seventh century the Venerable Bede set down his account of the history of the Church in England.

Along the seaboard of the counties of Durham and Cleveland the industrial theme continues, but south of Teesside, where the Cleveland Hills come down to the sea, the coastal scenery changes. Cliffs back the little villages and there are rugged little inlets used for shelter by the fishermen and sailors frequenting this coast. Captain James Cook was a native of these parts and set off on his first journey round the world from Whitby, where the River Esk, flowing through its beautiful valley, reaches the sea. The port, with its little houses pressed against the cliffs, on which the ruins of Whitby Abbey rise magnificently, has a genuine seafaring atmosphere, with fishing boats and all the accoutrements of their activity lined up along the quay. Whitby Abbey dates back to the seventh century and was the home of Caedmon, the monk and poet. Like many east-coast churches, the abbey was sacked by the Danes, and rebuilt after the Norman Conquest. Another little fishing village farther south, whose narrow streets slope steeply down to the sea, is Robin Hood's Bay. There is a splendid sandy bay three miles (5 km) long here which attracts thousands of summer visitors. At its southern end is Ravenscar, from whose high cliffs there are lovely views of the coast. The Cleveland Coast Path, which has been used since Roman times, and probably before, is now a long-distance coast walk and runs along the cliffs here.

The star of the Yorkshire coastal resorts is Scarborough, a very attractive town built on cliffs, below which stretches a good sandy beach. Scarborough could be

Right: The Blackpool Illuminations are one of the end-of-season highspots of this lively Lancashire seaside resort. Trams still ply up and down the promenade and are lit up during the Illuminations. Soaring above the sea front, the Blackpool Tower provides a bird's-eye view of town and sea.

Overleaf: Port Erin lies at the south-western end of the Isle of Man and has some fine coastal scenery and a good beach. Though part of Britain, the Isle of Man is constitutionally separate and has its own coinage and its own legislature in the Courts of Tynwald.

Right: The old harbour of Scarborough nestles under the promontory on which stands the Church of St. Mary, where Anne Brontë is buried, and the keep of the twelfth-century castle. The elegant old spa stretches south above the cliff gardens and the beach

Below: The graceful Humber Bridge connects the north and south parts of Humberside which are separated by the River Humber. On the north side of the river is Kingston-upon-Hull, an important seaport trading with northern Europe.

considered the first English seaside resort, for there is evidence in an old engraving that there were bathers on the Scarborough beach even in the seventeenth century. Its popularity grew in the nineteenth century when the railway arrived, and the fact that it offered the health-giving properties of mineral waters, as well as sea bathing, gave it a special attraction.

The mineral spa still survives on the front, and the beach is well patronized by bathers, but Scarborough has developed many other attractions. Among them are a fun fair at the harbour end of the town, above which are the remains of Scarborough Castle, a fine Italianate garden on the cliffs to the south, a theatre, many restaurants and all the other attractions of a modern seaside resort.

From here south to Spurn Head, at the mouth of the Humber, the coast receives a perpetual hammering from the sea, which is gradually eroding it away. It will be a long time before the cliffs and sandy bays disappear, however, and in the meantime they are enjoyed by thousands of visitors from the industrial hinterland at resorts like Filey, where the caravans and holidy-camp chalets stand in seemingly endless rows above the bay. Some of the most spectacular cliffs of the east coast lie along here near Bempton and culminate in Flamborough Head, once a popular place for Viking landings, and today the nesting ground of sea birds. On the southern side of the Head is Bridlington, a resort as popular as Filey and with the added attraction of a Georgian mansion and park, Sewerby Hall, to visit.

As the land slopes gently down to Spurn Head, farmland takes over. In their centre, at Sproatley, is Burton Constable Hall, a handsome Tudor building and one of many that were built in that part of the Wolds that lie behind the seashore and the Vale of York beyond.

Walkers can explore the North York Moors, whose rolling countryside stretches north-west to the Cleveland Hills, by following the 37 miles of footpath which make up the Rosedale Circuit. As its name suggests, the village of Rosedale Abbey has the remains of an old abbey.

North York Moors and the Wolds

Behind the sea coast of Yorkshire and Cleveland lie hills and moors which block the eastward passage of the rivers, forcing them to flow west and into the Vale of York before finding their way back to the east coast. These highland areas are the Cleveland Hills in the north, the Hambleton Hills to the west, the Yorkshire moors and the Wolds to the south. Though small in area they have a special beauty with their smooth green slopes broken by stone walls, wind-blown trees around isolated farmhouses, and desolate moors – all the atmosphere, in fact, of Emily Brontë's book *Wuthering Heights*, set in South Yorkshire moorland.

The Lyke Wake Walk, which starts in the Cleveland Hills and crosses the moors to the coast, where it joins the Cleveland Way, gives many fine and lonely views across the northern moors, though there are also minor roads leading to the choicest spots. Among them, in the centre of the moors, is Rosedale Abbey, a small village in Rosedale taking its name from the Cistercian nunnery that once flourished here. The Seven, the stream that runs by it, like many that cut through the moors, flows south into the Vale of Pickering, which separates the moors from the Wolds and where many fine towns, pretty villages and the once great abbeys of this part of Yorkshire lie.

Perhaps the greatest of these is above the River Rye near Helmsley, a fine market town complete with castle to the west of the vale. Rievaulx, a splendid twelfth-century Cistercian monastery, though ruined, still rises three storeys above its clearing in the wood-covered hills. South of Helmsley, where the Vale of York climbs up towards the Hambleton Hills, is Coxwold, where Shandy Hall was the home of Laurence Sterne, who preached in the village church and named his brilliant *Tristram Shandy* after his home. Newburgh Priory, near Coxwold, is another abbey, but this has been incorporated into a mansion, parts of which are Elizabethan. Oliver Cromwell's body is said to lie here in a bricked-up tomb which has never been opened.

In the Vale of Pickering itself is one of the grandest of all English mansions, Castle Howard, designed by Sir John Vanbrugh in 1699. The great domed building with its grandly furnished interiors and priceless picture collection is surrounded by green lawns and trees and overlooks an extensive artificial lake. Nearby, on the River Derwent, is Kirkham Priory, the still impressive ruin of a once large Augustinian priory. Here the Vale of Pickering enters the Vale of York, a valley into which flow the rivers from the Pennines whose valleys make up the beautiful Yorkshire Dales.

The Yorkshire Wolds, lying between the Vale of York and the sea, have a distinctive character. They are low, undulating hills with rich farmlands where sheep graze. There is nothing dramatic about this scenery, but it evidently pleased at least one Tudor family, for they built their magnificent home, Burton Agnes Hall, at the charming village of this name. The hall is most impressively set in a formal garden and includes among its possessions a collection of Impressionist paintings and works by Cézanne and Matisse.

The Pennines

The glory of Yorkshire is the Pennine ridge which, beginning in the smoky industrial world of south Yorkshire, strides over northern England towards the Scottish border in ever-increasing wildness. Off the slopes of this mountain ridge green valleys run east to the Vale of York, their upper slopes rising to the stony wilderness of the watersheds that separate them; on the valley floors abbeys and mansions stand in their rich estates guarded by castles on higher ground.

This has always been a rich land. Before the Romans came, men set up communities on the lower slopes of the Pennines, leaving mysterious stone circles for posterity to puzzle over. The Romans made York their headquarters and mined the ores and collected the wool off the sheep that thrived on the grassy hills. During the Middle Ages the northern tribes and the kings and barons of the south turned York into a battlefield, and the land was laid waste. Castles were built to establish the rule of law and order and the woollen trade revived. When the industrial age arrived, the towns along the Pennines, using the waters of the many streams which flow down from them, began to supply the whole world with Yorkshire-manufactured woollens. Leeds, at the southern end of the Pennines on the River Aire, became the centre of the woollen trade; Halifax expanded its position as the leading town in cloth manufacture; Wakefield produced clothing; and Bradford, where J. B. Priestley was born, and which still has an important wool exchange, grew rich on worsted. The sprawling mass of industrial towns is still there today, but immediately to the north nature takes over, erasing all memory of 'dark, satanic mills' as one penetrates the upper reaches of the Yorkshire Dales.

The dales are valleys carved out by rivers that begin their lives in the high Pennines and find their way to the River Ouse, which flows through the Vale of York. The Aire, on which Leeds lies, created Airedale, which has given its name to a lively Yorkshire terrier used originally for otter hunting. One of the Aire's tributaries, the River Worth, leads to a small hill village called Haworth, known to all the world as the home of the Brontë sisters, who drew inspiration from the moors that surrounded them for their romantic novels. Higher up, near its

Vanbrugh and Hawksmoor, the great eighteenth-century architects, designed Castle Howard in the grandiose Baroque style. This lavish palace, built for the Earl of Carlisle, has a splendid park in which are a family mausoleum, a temple, obelisks and other architectural features.

source, the Aire passes through Skipton, where Clifford Castle guards the Aire
Gap, which allows passage across the Pennines and which was exploited by the
builers of the Leeds-Liverpool Canal in the nineteenth century.

To the north of the Aire as it approaches Leeds is Ilkley Moor, scene of the
traditional song that recounts how a man who went on the moors without a hat
('baht 'at') caught cold, died and was devoured by worms, which were eaten by
ducks, which provided a dinner for his friends. Ilkley lies on the River Wharfe
whose valley, Wharfedale, contains the ruins of splendid Bolton Abbey. The
abbey lies amid green fields where the valley narrows towards the upper reaches
and where the stone-cottage village of Grassington is found. This is good
walking territory, while pot-holers find plenty of caverns to explore along the
slopes of Great Whernside, which lies to the north of Wharfedale.

Ilkley lies in Wharfedale to the north of the industrial conurbations of Leeds and Bradford. The moors above the town rise to 1,320 feet (400 m) and provide lovely views of the dale from a point quaintly named the Cow and Calf Rocks.

West of Wharfedale, on the watershed which separates it from Ribblesdale, which runs south-westwards to the Lancashire coast, is some of the wildest and most solitary Pennine country of this area. Malham, at its centre, is surrounded by steep rugged limestone hills; to the north of the village is Malham Cove, a spectacular amphitheatre of 240-foot-high (73-m) limestone cliffs which provide the backcloth for the setting of trees and stony stream below. Also nearby is Gordale Scar, a rocky ravine with waterfalls that pour over piles of shattered rocks, a scene which inspired the large painting by James Ward in London's Tate Gallery.

Nidderdale, to the north, runs from the north-east slopes of Great Whernside (2,310 feet/704 m). Knaresborough, built beside the River Nidd, is one of the more interesting Nidderdale towns, the narrow streets of its old town sheltering under a cliff on which stands the fourteenth-century castle. A female Nostradamus called Mother Shipton lived in Knaresborough around 1500 and prophesied, among other things, that the world would end in 1981. Close by is Harrogate, a nineteenth-century spa with good period architecture.

Near where the River Nidd joins the Ouse stands the great house of Beningborough Hall, just outside the city of York. This is a showplace of the National Trust, whose work preserves so much of England's heritage from neglect and destruction. Beningborough is an eighteenth-century house set in some 400 acres (162 hectares) of land, and continuing restoration has made it one of the best preserved in England. It houses a collection of pictures from the National Portrait Gallery.

The Ouse, before flowing through York, gathers in all the waters of the Nidd, Ure, and Swale. Romans, Danes and Normans built up this lovely city, which retains much of its medieval character in its walls, gates and timbered houses, especially in the narrow Shambles. York's Minster, a view of which must be the highspot of any visit to York, is thought by many to be the most beautiful cathedral in England. It took two centuries to build and is renowned for its stained glass. York is also the site of Britain's main railway museum.

Travelling north-west up the Ure Valley from York one arrives at Ripon, which is also famous for its fine cathedral, built on a site where there has been Christian worship since the seventh century. The Saxon crypt of St. Wilfrid's church remains in the present building. Just two miles (3 km) to the south is Fountains Abbey, a Cistercian monastery founded in 1132 and owing much of its splendour to the fact that its monks became rich through the wool trade. Fountains is one of the most beautiful and best preserved abbeys in the country.

From Ripon, the river valley leads up into Wensleydale, among the most famous of all the Yorkshire Dales, if only for the famous cheese that it produces. But there are far greater treasures than this in the valley of the Ure. Jervaulx Abbey lies just east of where the Ure Valley becomes Wensleydale. Like Fountains and Rievaulx, this was a twelfth-century abbey deprived of its power by Henry VIII's decision to destroy the monastic system which challenged his own authority. The proximity of three such powerful monasteries in an area important economically and politically in the life of the country attracted his early attention.

Imposing Barnard Castle guarded the road across the Pennines from Richmond to Penrith. It was built in the twelfth century by Bernard Baliol. When Dickens visited the village below the castle he was inspired by a clock-making shop to write **Master Humphrey's Clock**.

The presence of castles in the area also denotes its importance; Middleham Castle, at Middleham, to the north-west of Jervaulx Abbey, was owned by Richard III, and Bolton Castle, on the north side of Wensleydale, was Mary Queen of Scots' prison in 1568. Where the Swale leaves its hilly valley and enters the Vale of York the entrance is guarded by Richmond's castle, which has a panoramic view of the vale and the Cleveland Hills beyond. There is an abbey here too, for a mile (1.6 km) to the south-east of the town is Easby Abbey, whose remains include a well-preserved refectory and monks' infirmary.

Guarding the northern entrances into the Yorkshire Vale is Barnard Castle in County Durham, which also enjoys superb Pennine scenery on its western side. The Durham moors, through which flow the Tees, the Wear and the Derwent, are as wild as any on the Pennine Chain and rise to 2,780 feet (847 m) on the Milburn Forest overlooking the River Eden, which flows between the Pennines and the Cumbrian Mountains.

On the Tees lies one of the most spectacular waterfalls in England, High Force, where the water is squeezed between sheer rock walls and falls in a foaming torrent over the Great Whin escarpment. To the west is the highest English waterfall, at Caldron Snout, a mile (1.6 km) from the nearest minor road but worth the walk especially after rain. In these parts rain falls frequently, making life difficult for the walkers and motorists who are becoming increasingly aware of the beauties of this unspoiled and, until recently, relatively unvisited part of England.

The Lake District

The distance from the Irish Sea coast across to the valley of the River Eden, which separates the Lake District of north-west England from the Pennines, is hardly more than 20 miles (32 km), yet in this short distance there are mountains that rise to more than 3,000 feet (914 m), and breathtaking landscapes whose beauty makes Lakeland one of the most popular holiday areas in Britain. Wild rocky slopes, smiling green valleys, bare mountain tops, deep blue tarns, cascading streams, forests, moorland, the paths of Ice Age glaciers and rocks forced up through the earth's crust by volcanic action, all contribute to the dramatic and varied scenery to be enjoyed here.

It is interesting to reflect that the beauty of the area was not properly appreciated until the great Romantic movement of the nineteenth century, when the writings of the poets associated with the lakes opened people's eyes to the wonders that lay hidden in the Cumbrian mountains. It was Wordsworth, with his Englishness and his deep feeling for nature, who did more than anyone else to popularize the lakes. With the coming of the railways in the 1840s, the destiny of Lakeland as a major tourist attraction was decided.

Wordsworth and his sister, Dorothy, lived at Grasmere and at Rydal Water, both little lakes at the northern end of Windermere, the largest lake in Cumbria and in England. Thus they were at the very heart of Lakeland, for this is at the foot of the great mass of mountains which include 3,210-foot (978-m) Scafell Pike, England's highest peak, 3,118-foot (950-m) Helvellyn, one of the most popular climbs in lakeland, and Great Gable (2,949 feet/899 m), from which many of the rivers that feed the lakes flow.

Grasmere and Rydal Water are fed by the River Rydal, which flows from the mountains to the north. Grasmere, with its wooded banks, is an extremely pretty lake, and the village, with its stone walls, cottages and streets overhung with trees, is idyllic. Wordsworth lived at Dove Cottage, now a museum, when he first arrived in Lakeland. His sister lived with him, and the writer De Quincey was often his guest and later his tenant when Wordsworth moved after his marriage.

Ambleside is a larger village on the edge of a wood through which several streams flow into Lake Windermere. It is second only in importance to the town of Windermere as a holiday centre and therefore crowded during the summer months. There is a National Trust Information Centre and many facilities for sporting activities, including guides and equipment for would-be mountaineers.

Lake Windermere stretches south of Ambleside for ten miles (16 km), with low, wooded hills on each bank except at Claife Heights on the west bank opposite Windermere town, from which one can look down over the islands in this part of the lake. The famous children's storyteller and illustrator Beatrix Potter lived on the southern edge of Claife Heights at Sawrey, drawing much of her inspiration from the country around her. Windermere itself is a busy resort halfway along the east bank of the lake, with hotels, places of entertainment and a steamer landing stage, from which there are trips round the lake and boats for hire. At the southern end of the lake is Lakeside, one of the many adventure holiday centres of the area, where sailing, canoeing, hillwalking, climbing and many other sports are available.

Overleaf: Towering behind Blea Tarn Farm, Bowfell lies in the glorious mountainous centre of the Lake District, and from its 2,960-foot (902-m) summit there are views of Scafell, Langdale Pikes and Skiddaw.

Between Windermere and Coniston Water to the west lies the Grizedale Forest, a wooded area overlooking Coniston, the lake on which Donald Campbell was killed while attempting to break the world's water speed record in 1967. Another famous name connected with Coniston is that of John Ruskin, whose grave is in the parish church and some of whose pictures and other relics can be seen at the Ruskin Museum in Coniston village.

To the north and approachable by road from Ambleside lie the great mountains of Great Gable and Scafell. The Langdale road goes up a pretty wooded valley to Middle Fell, the junction of two valleys, Mickleden and Oxendale. Both of these have paths leading up to the summits and meeting at Angle Tarn, a small lake surrounded by the austere grandeur of bare mountain slopes, and not to be confused with Angle Tarn near Patterdale. Above, to the south-west, lies Scafell and ahead Great Gable, from both of which there are exciting views of rocky slopes, with gulleys and ravines that dive down to the valley floor. Farther afield from Scafell Pike the views extend to the Irish Sea, with the Isle of Man visible on clear days and all the nearby peaks and dales of the southern area of the Lake District readily picked out. To the west of Scafell the land drops into a wilderness of rock, amid which lies Wast Water, with its enormous screes sliding down its east side and a road picking its way through the rocky landscape on the west. This road can only be approached from the west by taking the Hardknott Pass from Ambleside to Eskdale Green.

To the north of Ambleside the road climbs up the Rothay valley and then down to Thirlmere, to the east of which rise the majestic slopes of Helvellyn. The best approach to the mountain, whose crescent-shaped summit embraces a small lake far below, is from Patterdale, but there are paths from Thirlmere, notably up Helvellyn Gill.

The open valley north of Thirlmere leads to Keswick, north of which looms the rounded shape of 3,054-foot (931-m) Skiddaw. Keswick is a large town on the River Greta and a centre for visiting the northern lakes of Cumbria. The Keswick area was the home of the Herries family of the Hugh Walpole novels, which recount the story of a Cumbrian family over several generations. In the centre of Keswick is a Moot, or meeting hall, of the early nineteenth century; St. Johns churchyard, which has lovely views over Derwent Water, is where Hugh Walpole is buried.

Right: Derwent Water is one of the loveliest of the English lakes, and its tree-covered islands add to its charm. At its northern end is Keswick, a popular rendezvous for walkers in summer and skiers who frequent the slopes of Skiddaw in winter. To the south is beautiful Borrowdale.

The Langdale Pikes provide a distinctive outline on the horizon for walkers descending from Sty Head Pass. This is a bleak crossing point for climbers on their way to conquer some of England's most formidable peaks. Among those surrounding it are Scafell Pike, the highest at 3,210 feet (978 m), Great Gable, and Pillar.

From Derwent Water the River Derwent flows north across a wide green valley, with Skiddaw providing a magnificent backcloth to the north-east and the wooded slopes of Thornthwaite Forest to the west. The valley of Bassenthwaite lake stretches out into green fields and the coastal plain at its northern end, with the River Derwent flowing through Cockermouth, Wordsworth's birthplace, on its way to the sea.

At the southern end of Derwent Water the road rises over Borrowdale, from whose wooded and bracken-covered slopes there are some spectacular views of the lake with its wooded island and Skiddaw beyond. At the top of the hill the valley opens up with fine views of the Borrowdale Fells, and continuing west up the Honister Pass there are views of Great Gable to the south. The pass leads over what was once a hazardous road to Buttermere, a pretty lake from whose edge hill-slopes covered in bracken and grass climb smoothly up to High Stile (2,633 feet/803 m) and Red Pike (2,479 feet/756 m). A stream links Buttermere to Crummock Water, which is fringed by the Grasmoor Fells to the north-east.

Left: From Skiddaw there are fine views of Derwent Water and the surrounding fells and of Helvellyn, which lies to the south alongside Thirlmere. On a clear day the Isle of Man is visible to the west.

At the head of Crummock Water the Cocker flows north to Cockermouth, and a valley to the west leads to Lowes Water, a small lake set amid farmlands. The road past here leads to Ennerdale Water, which lies to the south-west of Crummock Water. This is a dead-end valley, like many of those leading into the Great Gable massif, and its upper part has been taken over by the Forestry Commission, so entrance is limited for cars, which cannot get all the way to the lake; one must walk the last half mile (800 m) or so.

From Keswick the road leads eastward to Ullswater, for the High Fells stand in the way, and one has to follow the Penrith Road, turning south up Troutbeck for the road that leads over the fells to central Ullswater. This is a splendid lake with fine mountains all round. To the west, from the valley entrance at Aird Beck, where a waterfall plunges some 70 feet (21 m) over a steep drop, the lake is at its best, with all the wild character of Wast Water but with woods and a lovely green vale as well.

Ullswater is a long, curving lake whose south-western end lies to the east of Helvellyn. Patterdale stretches to the south and is a popular starting point for walks to Helvellyn, Keswick and Hawes Water.

The Goldrill Beck runs over a stony bed down Patterdale to the tiny village, which is a popular starting point for the walk up Grisedale to the Striding Edge route up Helvellyn.

On the south-east side of the lake is Place Fell, a good place from which to view the mountains on the north-west side. Patterdale, lying at the end of the lake, is a neat little village used as a base by climbers intent on tackling Helvellyn, as the most popular routes for the ascent of the mountain begin here. There are several routes, ranging from the easy, but longer, pony track to the shorter and dramatic one which ascends to the summit along the narrow watershed known as Striding Edge, which has steep drops to each side and a scramble over loose stones near the summit.

To the south of Ullswater lies another isolated lake, Hawes Water. To reach this by road requires yet another long detour. This is not uncommon in the Lake District, where a distance, short as the crow flies, is often increased many times by roads which must skirt lakes and hills. Most people walk to Hawes Water from Howtown on Ullswater's southern banks, to which there is a road and steamers from Pooley Bridge. A short walk up Fusedale Beck brings one to the lake. Once a relatively small lake, Hawes Water was converted into a reservoir by the construction of a dam at its northern end in 1937. Below its waters now lie the remains of Mardale village, including a pub, the ruins of a church and several farms. The fate of Hawes Water reminds one that the lakes of Cumbria, like the Welsh lakes, fulfil a useful purpose for, as well as satisfying their visitors' thirst for relaxation in beautiful surroundings, they provide water for many northern towns.

Border Country

The northernmost counties of England have always been disputed territory, first between the Romans and the Picts and Scots, and later between the kingdoms of England and Scotland. The Roman wall which runs from Wallsend, east of Newcastle-upon-Tyne, to the Solway Firth, is a symbol of the belligerent history of these Border Counties.

The largest town on the wall today is Carlisle, in Cumbria, though here the Roman remains are mostly buried under the later city, except for parts of the wall which can be seen to the east of the city. William II built the castle at the northern end of the town in 1092, and the building of the Citadel, farther south by today's railway station, was ordered by Henry VIII. The wall on the west side of Carlisle, overlooking the Caldew River, is medieval. The small red-sandstone cathedral, founded as a Norman priory, was destroyed by Cromwell's troops, and what remains is now a memorial chapel for the Border Regiment.

Carlisle lies on the northern bank of King Water, a tributary of the Eden which flows out into the Solway Firth. King Water rises in the Spadeadam Forest, itself just the south-west corner of the vast Border Forest Park that also includes the Kielder and Wark Forests, which is one of the largest man-planted forests in Europe. Kielder Castle, a former hunting lodge of the Dukes of Northumberland in the centre of Kielder Forest, is now an information centre which supplies advice on the many waymarked paths through the forest, where the Forestry Commission has also set up picnic and camping sites. The whole Border Forest Park forms the western border of the Northumberland National Park, nearly 400 square miles (1036 sq km) of hill, moorland and forest stretching to the Cheviot Hills.

Along the southern edge of the forest area the most interesting stretches of Hadrian's Wall are to be found. The road from Greenhead, where Thirlwall Castle was itself built from stone quarried from the wall in the fourteenth century, to Low Brunton follows the line of the Stanegate Road built along the wall by the Romans to service the seventeen great forts placed at regular intervals to house the garrisons and their bath-houses, kitchens and stores.

The emperor Hadrian suggested the building of the wall when he visited Britain in AD 122, intending that it should not only prevent attacks from the Scots to the north but also from bands of guerrillas wandering about the country to the south of the wall. Until it was finally evacuated in the fourth century, when the Roman Empire was crumbling and all available troops were needed at home, it was often visited by emperors, including Severus, Caracalla and, in the final years of the empire, Theodosius, who strengthened and reformed it in an effort to subdue the barbarian Picts, Scots and Saxons who from time to time succeeded in overrunning it.

At Housesteads, about halfway between Greenhead and Chollerton, where quite an amount of the Roman fort has been excavated, there is a small museum; here one can walk along the wall imagining as one stares across the empty hills what it must have been like for some unhappy foreign legionary who had been pressed into service for the Roman armies. The last visible section of wall lies at Heddon-on-the-Wall, seven miles (11 km) west of Newcastle, where at the Black

Gate Museum may be seen a model of the whole wall and items excavated from it.

In this hotly contested part of Britain, where the wars and skirmishes with the Scots continued until England and Scotland were joined together under one king, and where there was also a struggle for power between the Percy family, Earls and Dukes of Northumberland, and the English kings, the easiest routes through the country were by the coastal plain and up the river valleys which penetrated the Cheviot Hills. It is here therefore one finds many places of major interest.

One of the most bitterly contested of all the towns in this region was Berwick-upon-Tweed, which was finally won for England in 1482 by the Duke of Gloucester, later Richard III, during the reign of his brother Edward IV, though real union did not take place until James VI of Scotland became James I of England as well. In spirit, Berwick remains a Scottish town, as any visitor will attest. Its wall surrounding the solid grey houses, the three bridges that cross the River Tweed to the south, the 'English' side, and the castle, partly blown up to make way for the railway station, all give this very interesting place the air of a frontier town which has somehow ended up on the wrong side of the border.

Along the coast to the south lies another part of Northumberland with a special place in English history. This is Lindisfarne, or Holy Island, an island lying out to sea across tidal flats. From the crossing point at Beal it looks flat and uninteresting, which is perhaps the reason why the monks who built Lindisfarne Priory, aware of the greedy eyes of Viking and Dane, chose it. To reach the island today one drives or walks across the metalled causeway, first taking good note of the tide table posted there, for the tide comes in across the causeway with surprising speed. The causeway leads through sand dunes into the village of Lindisfarne, where the visitor is immediately touched by the atmosphere of peaceful tranquillity which reigns over the few small cottages and the ruins of the

Housesteads was one of the major Roman forts on Hadrian's Wall which crossed England from Carlisle to Newcastle. In the remains of the fort a museum displays the archaeological finds in the area.

abbey. Through the empty windows of the abbey one can see the curving shore with its upturned boats used as storehouses by the fishermen, and the shattered cone of Lindisfarne Castle.

The story of Lindisfarne began in the seventh century when King Oswald asked the monks of Iona to set up a monastery in Northumbria. At first little was done, but when Aidan arrived and chose Lindisfarne as the site for the monastery the Christian community began to grow and spread its works throughout Northumbria. The most important of the subsequent bishops to run Lindisfarne was Cuthbert, whose body now lies in Durham Cathedral. The greatest relic of the life of the priory is the magnificent Lindisfarne Gospels, written and illuminated at Lindisfarne in honour of St. Cuthbert in about 698. It is now in the British Library in London.

The ruins one sees today are those of the Norman priory of 1093, with its subsequent additions; the adjacent church of St. Mary was founded in the same period. Much of the stone of the priory was plundered for the building of Lindisfarne Castle in the sixteenth century. The castle had fallen into ruins by the nineteenth century, and the well-maintained building one sees today is largely the work of Sir Edward Lutyens.

To the south-west of Lindisfarne lies a small island to which St. Cuthbert is said to have escaped for periods of meditation. Another isolated group of islands he frequented is the Farne Islands, 2–5 miles (3–8 km) off the coast between Bamburgh and Seahouses, where a chapel built after his residence there has withstood the sea and gales for at least 500 years. While on the islands, Cuthbert studied the habits of the many thousands of sea birds that live on their protected shores and wrote a paper on the care of eider chicks. The Farne Islands may be visited today by boat from the port of Seahouses, from where trips to the islands' grey seal colonies are also popular.

Lindisfarne Castle stands guard over Holy Island, where St. Aidan founded a monastery in AD 635. In this isolated spot in the north-east of England, the monks kept learning and Christianity alive during Europe's Dark Age.

153

Seahouses is an attractive port on the north-east coast, where fishing boats and ferries to the Farne Islands crowd the small harbour. Farther up the coast is Bamburgh, with its impressive castle which towers over the village where Grace Darling, the heroine of a celebrated local sea rescue, is buried.

In strong contrast to Lindisfarne and its meditative and spiritual air is Bamburgh Castle, farther south at Bamburgh between Lindisfarne and Seahouses and perched on a titanic crag. Although much restored, it still seems formidable, a sight to have made even the most aggressive attackers quail. The castle withstood the Norsemen in the pre-Norman Period and was improved and strengthened by Henry I. It was besieged during the Wars of the Roses but survived until the nineteenth century, when it was restored by the family of the present owners. In the castle one can see St. Oswald's Chapel, which has Norman foundations and eighteenth-century walls, the armoury, and the keep built by Henry II.

Bamburgh is without doubt one of the showplaces of the Northumberland coast. Its sandy beaches stretch for miles, and the village that lies behind the castle is as charming as the castle is awesome. Bamburgh was the birthplace of the heroine Grace Darling, who, with her father, rowed out in a boat, locally called a 'coble', to rescue the passengers and crew of the steamer *Forfarshire* in a violent storm in 1838. This courageous deed has become legendary, and the Grace Darling Museum in Bamburgh tells the full story, as well as exhibiting the actual boat used in the rescue.

The Northumberland shoreline, as well as having superb beaches, is a
fishermen's coast where kippers, when herrings are plentiful, created a local
industry. At Craster the herrings are smoked over oak fires and are nationally
famous as 'Craster Kippers'. Today the industry is still carried on among the
sheds and little cottages above the tiny harbour. From Craster there is a cliff walk
to the north where Dunstanburgh Castle, which inspired several of Turner's
paintings, stands gaunt and tall above a cliff. Dunstanburgh was another of the
many castles built originally to repel invaders both from the north and the sea
and which in a later age inspired painters of romantic scenes. Alnwick Castle,
farther south and inland, was another, being painted by Canaletto, whose work
hangs in the castle.

Alnwick was the principal stronghold of the Percys, Earls and Dukes of
Northumberland, who still occupy it. They were not only powerful border lords
but strong enough to challenge the authority of the King of England. The family
came to grief, however, when Henry Bolingbroke (Henry IV) arrived to drive
Richard II from the throne of England. Shakespeare recorded the fall in the
fortunes of the Percy family through the character of Harry Hotspur in *Henry IV*,
Part I. The castle fell into ruins after the loss of Percy power and was rebuilt by
the Duke of Northumberland in the nineteenth century. Though inland, Alnwick
has a port at Alnmouth, an attractive village with a pleasant Victorian
atmosphere.

Another castle, along the River Coquet a few miles to the south, is
Warkworth, Harry Hotspur's birthplace. The castle is wonderfully situated on a
small hill above the town of neat grey houses, which climb up the green slopes
surrounding it. The River Coquet flows round the town and has an unusual
fortified medieval bridge; upriver and accessible by boat or towpath is a hermit's
cave.

The River Coquet, born near the Scottish border, flows down from the moors
of the Northumberland National Park, a wild and empty area with one or two
isolated clusters of buildings. Most of the inhabitants lived and still live in the
Coquet valley, and there are fine buildings along its length. At Brinkburn the

Durham Cathedral, built on a promontory round which flows the River Wear, is the most impressive medieval church in Britain. The body of St. Cuthbert was brought here by St. Aidan when Lindisfarne was overrun by the Danes in AD 883.

abbey is twelfth century, though not much remains of the original priory except the church. Farther upstream is Cragside, once the home of the Lord Armstrong who restored Bamburgh Castle; still deeper in the moors is Harbottle, where there was once a great Norman castle, now reduced to a few ruined walls. Near Harbottle is Holystone, a well considered to be of great medicinal value by the Romans and later by Christians, who founded a priory of Augustinian nuns there.

At Newbiggin-by-the-Sea, a resort for the busy industrial area of Tyneside, the character of the Border coast changes, and commercial ports alternate with popular resorts around Tynemouth, South Shields and Sunderland. Inland, the hills begin their descent to the great plain in which the rivers Tees and Wear wend their way to the sea and where the city of Durham stands, its castle and magnificent Norman cathedral dominating a 70-foot-high (21-m) wooded bluff above the Wear, surely one of the most impressive sights in all England.

Scotland

Scotland can be divided into three main areas: the Highlands to the north, which start abruptly just north of a line drawn between the Firth of Clyde on the west coast and the town of Stonehaven on the east and passing through Stirling in the centre, and which are themselves further divided by the Great Glen; the Lowlands, in the narrow waist of industrial area between Glasgow and Edinburgh; and the Southern Uplands, between the Galloway Peninsula and Berwick-upon-Tweed.

No other part of Britain has the spacious and rugged beauty of the Scottish Highlands. This is a land of apparently enormous distances, with great mountains that rise from the heather-covered slopes where a stalker who looks after the herds of deer may be the only person in sight, which is not surprising in an area where the population is less than 50 persons per square mile (19 per sq km) and

Rising to 2,399 feet (731 m), Suilven is one of the mountains in the Inverpolly National Nature Reserve north of Ullapool, on Scotland's rugged west coast. This exceptionally beautiful region can be reached by a minor road which circles it and other mountains in the area, such as Cul Mor, Cul Beag, Canisp and the craggy cone of Stac Polly.

often less than ten (4 per sq km). It is also a land of long sea inlets and inland lakes, both known as lochs, of seals and sea birds and, above all, of legends.

The Southern Uplands have their legends too, often concerned with the border wars against the English, and the castles and abbeys of the region have a more lived-in appearance than the desolate and solitary ruins of the north. There are more towns here, especially on the eastern side along the Tweed valley and its tributaries, where wool has been an important trade since medieval times. The western side of the Southern Uplands is a solitary area once again, with miles of empty hills stretching away to the horizon, and rivers that flow down through forested valleys to the Solway Firth.

The whole of the west coast of Scotland, with its peninsulas and islands, is yet another world, a world of Viking memories, of clan warfare and of breathtaking views of rugged coasts and restless seas.

Loch Dungeon nestles away from motor roads among the Rhinns of Kells, a range of mountains rising to 2,600 feet (792 m) which lie along the Galloway Forest Park in the western part of the Southern Uplands. It was across this wild country that Mary Queen of Scots fled after her defeat at Langside and that young Lochinvar rode to save his loved one from a forced marriage.

Southern Uplands

South of the Central Lowlands of Scotland there is a beautiful and romantic hilly region of vast grass-covered slopes and wild moors broken by rich valleys, in which streams tumble over rocky beds and the salmon rest in shady pools during their long journeys to the spawning grounds. This is the Southern Uplands, a land of poets and daring border raiders, of monks and magicians.

Most visitors to Scotland know the valley of the Tweed, with its ancient towns, rich in the history of border warfare, its superb salmon fishing and its famous cloth industry, but those who know the Southern Uplands well will tell you that their western end in Dumfries and Galloway is every bit as beautiful and has just as turbulent a history. This is the area of the Scottish dales: smooth, grass-covered valleys rising to moorlands which, though they smile in summer, can be just as cruel as the wild lands of Sutherland and the far north in winter.

The two aspects of the Uplands have inspired ballads that combine the sentiment and poignancy expressed in old Scottish songs or the poems of Robert Burns. Burns lived at Ayr, where the cottage in which he was born at Alloway is now a museum and the starting-off point for the Burns Heritage Trail, which takes in many of the places associated with Scotland's greatest poet, including Alloway Kirk, the Brig o' Doon and the Burns monument, all in Alloway, and the Tam o' Shanter Museum in Ayr.

Ayr is a large town lying by the sea in a landscape that lacks the drama of other parts of Scotland or the fire that burned in the poet himself. It seems strange to find Burns in such a peaceful spot, until one remembers that this was the coast on which the first Scots arriving from Ireland landed and began their gradual take over of Celtic territory, and that it is therefore a land of adventurous and restless people. The country around Ayr was a rich land where cattle and crops flourished, and it was fought over for centuries, a history to which the ruined castles and abbeys of the countryside attest. Near Ayr itself are two castles, Dundonald to the north and Dunure on the coast to the south. In the dungeon of the latter, the Commendator of Crossraguel Abbey was roasted alive by the fourth Earl of Cassillis, Lord of Dunure, who coveted the rich lands of the Cluniac abbey, whose impressive ruins may be visited near Maybole.

The coast to the north of Ayr is as famous for its many golf courses, including the championship course of Troon, as for the sandy beaches and mild climate which make it a major resort area. There are supernatural features about the coast to the south, notably the Witch of Ayr, who was supposed to have flown over the Carrick Hills and bewitched a spot known as the Electric Brae on the Dunure road. Here a car halted in its descent and left without its brakes on will climb slowly backwards up the hill. Realists say it is all an optical illusion created by the lie of the land; believers in the supernatural know better.

Opposite: Culzean Castle is the show-place of the west coast of Southern Scotland. It was built by the Kennedy clan in the late eighteenth century and designed by Robert Adam. Its huge park stretches to the sea cliffs. The top flat of the castle was presented to General Eisenhower in 1946 in recognition of his services to Britain.

Farther down the coast is famous Culzean Castle, actually an eighteenth-century house, but one designed on the grand scale by Robert Adam for the 10th Earl of Cassillis. And there is Ardstinchar Castle, a thirteenth-century stronghold near Ballantrae, whose Master was the inspiration for Robert Louis Stevenson's adventure story of the times of Bonnie Prince Charlie.

South of Ballantrae, Galloway comes to its western end at the strange hammerhead peninsula where steamers from Stranraer leave for Ireland and where, on its southern extremity, the last Pict leapt to his death rather than reveal the secret of the making of heather ale. Is this why Scots invented whisky?

The south-facing coast along the Solway Firth is intersected by rivers that flow down from the eastern end of the Southern Uplands. Between the Dee at Kirkcudbright, which runs south from Clatteringshaws Loch, and the River Cree, flowing from Loch Moan to Creetown to the west, are vast areas of forest – Cairn Edward, Kirkoughtree and Glentrool – and hills where sheep graze. To the east, the River Nith, which flows down Nithdale past the Lowther Hills, passes through Dumfries, an old royal burgh with a fifteenth-century bridge and the house where Burns wrote *Annie Laurie*, now a museum to the poet. At the mouth of the river is fourteenth-century Caerlaverock Castle, a seat of the Maxwell family besieged by Edward I of England in 1300. Nearby, along the marshy edges of the Firth, there is a wildfowl reserve where geese and duck stay during the winter months.

The River Annan flows down from the Tweedsmuir Hills. In its upper reaches lies the Devil's Beef Tub, an impressive amphitheatre of cliffs, and on its tributary, Moffat Water, is Scotland's highest waterfall, the Grey Mare's Tail, which drops 200 feet (61 m) among hills covered in grass and bracken.

As the Annan approaches the coast near Ecclefechan, it passes through the grounds of Hoddom Castle, which has a fine, square keep and attractive, wooded walks round the river. Nearby is the home of Thomas Carlyle and the school he attended.

The border with England begins at the extreme eastern end of the Solway Firth, at which point the land is flat and featureless, which is probably why the Romans defended this part of their kingdom with cavalry. Gretna Green lies here, surrounded by green fields and with its cottages looking much as they did when the village was the place for runaway border marriages by people from England. The smithy where the marriages took place is still there but now simply a tourist sight for, since 1940, marriage by simply declaring an intention to be wed before the blacksmith has been illegal.

The River Esk joins the Solway Firth just east of Gretna Green after its journey through the pretty valley of Eskdale; this is itself joined by Liddesdale

Above: Yarrow Water is a lovely stream in a green valley that once rang to the clash of swords and shields of border battles. Ruined Newark Castle, the setting of Sir Walter Scott's Lay of the Last Minstrel, lies along the river, and Bowhill, the home of the Scotts of Buccleuch, is at the junction of Yarrow Water and Ettrick Water near Selkirk. There is a fine collection of paintings in the house.

Left: Melrose Abbey stands in Melrose below the Eildon Hills on the River Tweed. The Cistercian monks who founded it in 1136 in the reign of King David created a beautiful complex of buildings which, however, suffered continual damage by English raiders from across the border. Tradition says that the heart of Robert the Bruce rests among the ruins.

near Canonbie. About five miles (8 km) upstream in Liddesdale, which runs along the English border, is the famous castle of Hermitage, one of the most dour castles in Scotland, situated as it is on an empty and bleak moor. In the fifteenth century the castle belonged to James, Earl of Bothwell, lover of Mary Queen of Scots, who made a famous ride to him across the moor from Jedburgh and back on hearing that Bothwell had been wounded during a border skirmish.

Jedburgh lies on a tributary of the River Teviot, which joins the Tweed at Kelso. This is the heart of the border country, where the many towns, castles and abbeys are evidence of its importance. Twelfth-century Jedburgh Abbey is well preserved and makes an impressive sight on its hillside above Jed Water. The town is built on the same hill, and its main street rises steeply to what was once the castle and is now the prison. It is an ideal centre for visiting the other notable towns, abbeys and castles in this part of the Tweed lowlands.

The Roman Road that runs near Jedburgh, and which can still be walked along in some sections, leads towards Melrose, a neat little town on the Tweed in the shadow of the Eildon Hills, whose three summits are supposed to have been split apart by the devil and below which lies the site of the Roman camp of Trimontium.

Apart from the Eildon Hills, said by legend to be the burial place of King Arthur and his knights as well as the place where the legendary Scottish magician Thomas the Rhymer received his powers of magic, the glory of Melrose is its Cistercian abbey, a splendid building destroyed many times during the border wars but rebuilt in the fourteenth and fifteenth centuries, though damaged again later. The abbey, notable for its traceried stonework, contains the heart of Robert the Bruce, and the museum has relics found in the Roman fort.

Nearby to the west, also on the Tweed, lies Abbotsford, the home of Sir Walter Scott, whose books romanticized Scottish history and became best-sellers. Scott's house is a typical nineteenth-century mock-baronial pile and contains a number of interesting exhibits, including a portrait head of Mary Queen of Scots painted the day after her execution.

To the east is Dryburgh Abbey, another of the four border abbeys founded in the reign of David I – the others are Jedburgh, Melrose and Kelso – which was destroyed by the English in 1544. The abbey's monastic buildings, including the cloisters, survive to give a vivid impression of the life of its monks in this sheltered and wooded curve of the River Tweed. Sir Walter Scott lies buried in the church.

Downriver lies Kelso, a town with an exceptionally large and handsome main square and the ruins of an important abbey. Like many border towns, Kelso also suffered frequently from English raids during the border wars. The Old Pretender was declared King James VIII in the market square here, and Bonnie Prince Charlie stayed in the town during his retreat, so Kelso was not very popular with the English even in later centuries. The splendid bridge over the Tweed gives a good view over the town and leads to what was once Roxburgh village and its mighty castle but is now no more than an evocative mound covered with trees and fragments of stone walls. From here, however, one can see Floors Castle across the valley and this splendid eighteenth-century mansion, with its surrounding park, makes up for the disappointing ruins of Roxburgh.

From Kelso the Tweed flows down to the North Sea at Berwick-upon-Tweed, no longer the disputed frontier with England but with all the characteristics of a Scottish town for all that. The frontier now lies to the north in empty ground near Lamberton.

Central Lowlands

Between the Southern Uplands of Scotland and the Highlands extends a broad band of flat land, at the western end of which are the Firth of Clyde and the city of Glasgow and at the eastern the Firth of Tay, the Firth of Forth and the city of Edinburgh, the word 'firth' indicating a broad sea inlet. Though this area does not claim to compete with the beauty of other parts of Scotland, it possesses many attractive places near the two great cities. From Glasgow it is a short drive to Loch Lomond and the Trossachs, and from Edinburgh to the south-east coast resorts of Scotland or across to the resorts of Fife is only a short distance.

Glasgow has never quite lived down its undeserved and today unjust reputation for being an ugly, smoke-grimed industrial city. The nineteenth-century industrialists left the city with some handsome architecture and a collection of works of art that any city can be proud of, and now that the slums have been cleared and the blackened face cleaned up, the city has emerged as its nineteenth-century builders must have envisaged it.

Glasgow's origins go back far beyond the nineteenth century, however, and it is St. Mungo to whom credit is given for its foundation in AD 543. His body is buried in the cathedral, which was founded in the twelfth century and is a fine example of medieval architecture. Glasgow first began to grow into a large shipping port in the seventeenth century, when the establishment of colonies in North America created a trade in such hitherto unknown substances as tobacco and sugar-cane, as well as in cotton, hides and timber. The Industrial Revolution, with its demand for steamships and engineering products, merely encouraged Glasgow's development.

The parts of Glasgow that date back to the period of shipping and commercial development include George Square, which was laid out in the eighteenth century, and the Royal Exchange, built in 1775 as a private merchant's house. Glasgow University, training ground for such famous Britons as James Boswell, Adam Smith, James Watt, Joseph Lister and David Livingstone, is today housed in Gilbert Scott's nineteenth-century neo-Gothic buildings on Gilmore Hill,

Above: Gourock stands at the point where the Clyde ceases to be a commercial estuary filled with the clangour of shipbuilding and becomes a sea loch flanked by green hills. Many of the great liners of the world once passed the Cloch Lighthouse, but now the traffic consists of freighters and ferries which serve the Kintyre Peninsula, the Isle of Arran and the Hebrides.

Right: Despite its popular appeal, Loch Lomond remains remarkably unspoiled, though the traffic along its west bank is heavy in summer. The southern part of the lake is open and full of islands, but in the north the mountains crowd in with Ben Lomond lording it over the others.

founded by papal dispensation in the fifteenth century. No such permission was required for the University of Strathclyde, which was established in 1964 and specializes in science and business studies.

Many of Glasgow's fine museums lie to the south of the city, notably Pollok House, which has one of the finest collections of Spanish paintings in Britain, and the Transport Museum in Albert Drive. The Glasgow City Art Gallery is on the north side of the river in Kelvingrove Park by the University.

Glaswegians are lucky to have some of the most popular beauty spots of Scotland on their doorstep. Loch Lomond, at 24 miles (39 km) from top to bottom the largest lake in Britain, is a mere 10 miles (16 km) away. In the south the loch is broad and dotted with pretty wooded islands, but as one drives north along the west bank the mountains close in and the summits of Ben Lomond and Ben Vorlich rise over 3,000 feet (over 900 m). The clans that ruled the loch were the Colquhouns and the MacGregors, one of whom, Rob Roy MacGregor, became the legendary Robin Hood of Scotland. At Tarbet, about halfway up the loch on the west bank, there is a pass westwards to Arrochar at the head of Loch Long, and beyond is Glen Croe, a mountainous corridor bordered by the Cobbler, as Ben Arthur mountain is called, and Ben Brock. The pass gives access to Loch Fyne and the Campbell-clan country around Inveraray.

To the east of Loch Lomond, and accessible only though Aberfoyle or Callander, lie the mountains of the Trossachs and Loch Katrine. This picturesque corner of Scotland, often called 'Glasgow's back garden,' suffers from almost too much popularity in the summer months, and the lovely little lochs among the pines are edged as much by parked cars and picnickers as by trees or grassy banks. Sir Walter Scott helped make the Trossachs fashionable with his poem *The Lady of the Lake*, and no-one would question that his inspiration was well founded.

Callander, to the east, lies along the southern edge of the Highlands and has justly been named the gateway to the Highlands, a title that it could share with Stirling to the south-east, whose castle broods over the plain below from a 250-foot (76-m) crag. Castles have stood on this rock since the eleventh century, and the present Stirling Castle dates from the fifteenth and sixteenth centuries. The infant Mary Queen of Scots was crowned in the Church of the Holy Rude below the castle and married Lord Darnley in the castle in 1565, but when her son James VI of Scotland became James I of England, the castle ceased to be a royal

Right: Kenmore lies in a beautiful wooded setting at the north-eastern end of Loch Tay on the southern edge of the Grampian Mountains. At the other end of the loch, to the south-west, is Killin, with the photogenic double falls of Dochart. Dominating the northern bank, the peak of Ben Lawers towers to 3,984 feet (1214 m).

*Below: Sir Walter Scott popularized Loch Katrine by including it in **The Lady of the Lake**, and today its eastern end is crowded in summer. The western end is equally beautiful and less easily accessible. This was the land of the MacGregor clan, whose most famous member was Rob Roy.*

residence. Two miles (3 km) to the south of Stirling is the site of the battle of Bannockburn in 1314, at which Robert the Bruce routed the English under Edward II. The site is now a property of the National Trust for Scotland, which maintains a visitor centre here, dominated by a statue of Robert the Bruce.

Stirling is a symbol of the old independent Scotland, both because of its identification with Robert the Bruce and the patriot William Wallace and because of its situation at the threshold of the Highlands. The city makes a powerful contrast with Edinburgh, 50 miles (80 km) away to the south-east which, despite its long history, has a freshness and entrepreneurial atmosphere about it that evokes the years of its growth during the eighteenth century after the Act of Union and the defeat of Bonnie Prince Charlie in 1745. Much of present-day Edinburgh's charm lies in the streets and squares of eighteenth-century buildings that lie parallel to the north of Princes Street. In Princes Street Gardens is an imposing monument to Sir Walter Scott, who brought about the first visit of a Hanoverian sovereign, George IV, to the city in 1822. The Gardens were created just before this visit by filling in the loch that lay under the rock on which stands the vast pile of Edinburgh Castle.

The rocky ridge of the Old City has a chain of streets linking the castle with the Palace of Holyroodhouse, where Mary Queen of Scots' secretary Rizzio was murdered. Known as the Royal Mile, these streets are full of interest, and the cathedral of St. Giles lies halfway along. Though founded in the twelfth century, most of the building was completed during the ensuing 300 years. It was from here that John Knox fulminated against Papal authority and introduced the more dour aspects of Scottish Protestantism to Scotland. In High Street, near the cathedral, is the house he is supposed to have inhabited.

The western or upper end of the Royal Mile, the Lawnmarket, was the section where farm folk sold their produce. It was also a fashionable area to live in, and there are some fine houses in the streets that wind steeply down to Princes Street Gardens. The Outlook Tower has a camera obscura in which a 360-degree panorama of Edinburgh is projected. Also in this area is Lady Stair's House, which contains objects that once belonged to such great Scottish literary figures as Robert Louis Stevenson, Robbie Burns and Sir Walter Scott.

The Lawnmarket climbs upwards to the castle, from which there are splendid views over the city. In its almost impregnable situation the castle has fended off attacks ever since the first Scots settled in Edinburgh. It was last attacked by Bonnie Prince Charlie, who, having taken the town, failed to take the castle, in which supporters of Hanoverian George II continued to defy the Young Pretender. The oldest part of the castle, and one spared by Robert the Bruce when he succeeded in taking the castle from the English in 1313, is St. Margaret's Chapel, named after its builder, the Saxon princess who became the wife of King Malcolm III and was canonized after her death in 1092. Mary Queen of Scots gave birth in 1566 to the future James I of England in the castle, the room in which he was born having his and his mother's initials carved on the ceiling. In the Crown Room of the palace part of the castle are kept the Scottish Crown Jewels which were hidden in Dunnottar Castle on the east coast during the wars of Cromwell's Commonwealth.

On the south side of Crown Square stands the old Parliament House, a splendid hall with a timbered roof, built in the fifteenth century and now used to show off some fine armour and other relics of the castle's history. More relics of Edinburgh's stirring history are on show at the Palace of Holyroodhouse end of the Royal Mile, and portraits of Scottish kings and other famous Scots can be seen at the National Portrait Gallery which, with the National Gallery of Scotland, contains many outstanding works of Scottish and international art.

Though Edinburgh is one of the most attractive cities in the world, the same cannot be said for its shoreline along the Firth of Forth, which has all the unpleasant features of most industrial areas until one reaches Seton Sands, where the wooded countryside leads down to sand dunes which are a gathering place for sea birds. At Berwick, at the mouth of the Firth of Forth, the beaches provide good bathing, and the little town, with its well-built cottages, is a popular summer resort. Off the coast rises the big mass of Bass Rock, and to the east are the extensive ruins of a former Douglas stronghold, Tantallon Castle.

Preceding pages: The Palace of Holyroodhouse in Edinburgh has a more romantic history than most. Mary Queen of Scots lived here after the death of her husband, the Dauphin of France; her favourite, David Rizzio, was murdered here; and she married Bothwell in the palace. Bonnie Prince Charlie held his court at Holyroodhouse, and Charles X of France spent some of his exile here.

Dunbar, farther along the coast, faces the North Sea and is a holiday centre with a long and romantic history. Edward I defeated the Scots here in 1296, but the fortunes of war were reversed when Edward II, fleeing from his defeat at Bannockburn in 1314, had to escape from Scotland by boat from Dunbar harbour. Mary Queen of Scots took refuge here with Darnley after the murder of Rizzio, and her third husband, Bothwell, was later made governor of the castle. In Cromwell's time Dunbar was severely damaged and the castle was used as a quarry for stones needed for the harbour. Today little remains of the castle except a few ruins on the headland, but the long High Street of the town has some attractive old houses, including the seventeenth-century Town House and Lauderdale House, designed by Robert Adam.

By the Water of Leith, in the northern part of Edinburgh is attractive Dean village, where mills ground the corn for Edinburgh's bakeries.

From here to the English border low cliffs border the sea and the countryside is given over to farms.

On the north side of the Firth of Forth, across the estuary from North Berwick, is Fife, occupying the peninsula that lies between the Firths of Forth and Tay. At Dunfermline, in the south, the Scottish kings had their home from the eleventh century until the union with England. In the centre of the peninsula is Loch Leven, where, on an island in the centre, is the castle which held Mary Queen of Scots prisoner and from which she escaped in 1568. Near Loch Leven, to the east, is Falkland Palace built by James IV and James V in the fourteenth and fifteenth centuries. This was the centre of royal life, and its French style suggests the influence of James V's French wives.

At the eastern end of the peninsula is St. Andrews, seat of the Royal and Ancient Golf Club, the arbiter of golfing rules, and a university town. On the cliffs above the sea are a ruined castle and the impressive walls of the ruined twelfth-century cathedral.

As on the east coast south of Edinburgh, the Fife coast has many small seaside resorts patronized by Edinburgh's inhabitants. Among these are those of the Neuk coast on the Firth of Forth west of the headland of Fife Ness.

The Forth Bridge ranks with the Eiffel Tower as an engineering marvel of the nineteenth century. The engineer Sir John Fowler designed it with two 1,710-foot (521-m) spans and two of 690 feet (210 m) in 1883 to carry the railway across the Firth of Forth.

The Great Glen

The great rift valley which separates the North-West Highlands of Scotland from the Grampian Highlands to the south-east, is known as the Great Glen of Alban, or Glen More. It has no passes on its south-eastern shore, except for Glen Spean and the coast roads out of Fort William and Inverness, but on its north-western bank there are glens that lead into some of the remotest parts of the Highlands. Along its 60-mile (97-km) length the glen contains three lochs, Ness, Oich and Lochy, joined since 1847 into one long waterway by Thomas Telford's Caledonian Canal, and is bounded for most of its length by many tarns. Britain's tallest mountain, 4,406-foot (1343-m) Ben Nevis, lies to the south of the Great Glen, near Fort William.

Until recently, the glen was a busy commercial channel linking the Irish Sea coast of Scotland to the North Sea but in recent times the traffic has declined, leaving the lochs and canals to pleasure boats that sail up and down between the wooded hills, past castles and villages, their crews keeping a lookout for the monsters that are said to lurk in Loch Ness and Loch Oich all the summer through.

At the south-western end of the glen, the Caledonian Canal passes through the flight of eight locks called Neptune's Staircase at Banavie, which takes northward-sailing boats along the canal to Loch Lochy. From the entrance to the loch a road leads south-east up to Spean Bridge and the glen that passes the splendid Commando Memorial, from where there are superb views of Ben Nevis and the glen leading to Fort William.

Crail, at the eastern end of Fife and facing the North Sea, has retained its character as an eighteenth-century fishing village. Today the fishermen devote themselves to lobster catching. The local church of St. Mary has relics which show that the Picts lived in Crail in the eighth century.

The Caledonian Canal, which links the lochs along the Great Glen, passes by Fort Augustus, where a fort was built in 1729 by General Wade. It was named Augustus after the Duke of Cumberland, whose ruthless tactics after the defeat of Bonnie Prince Charlie earned him the title of Butcher Cumberland. Fort Augustus is now an abbey with an impressive modern church.

Loch Lochy is a pretty stretch of water with trees and a steep ridge of mountains to the north. At its upper end the glen road crosses to the north-west side over the lock which lifts boats into Loch Oich. This small loch has a great many points of interest on its north-west bank.

The Road to the Isles begins up the valley leading to Loch Garry, a very wooded area with panoramic views. In front of a cluster of cottages before arriving at Glen Garry is a tall stone monument topped by an obelisk with seven carved heads. Below it a plaque tells the story of the two sons of the MacDonnells of Keppoch, a cadet branch of the MacDonnells of Glengarry, whose murder by seven kinsmen was avenged by the bard Iain Lom MacDonnell and James MacDonald of Sleat. They had the murderers killed, their heads cut off and washed in the stream which flows into Loch Oich near the monument, and then presented to the chief of Glengarry at his castle, Invergarry.

The ruins of Invergarry Castle, in which Bonnie Prince Charlie stayed before and after Culloden in 1746, rise grimly by the water's edge in the grounds of the splendid Glengarry Castle Hotel, which stands in beautiful grounds between the River Garry and Loch Oich.

Loch Oich is reputed to have a monster, older even than that of Loch Ness, though there are no hazy photographs of it to add fuel to the legend. The monster of Loch Ness is much more of a celebrity, and can be seen by imaginative people in the waters of the loch in the vicinity of Castle Urquhart, which is itself a most photogenic ruin built on a rock by the lake. Beyond the castle, at the head of little Urquhart Bay, is the village of Drumnadrochit at the entrance to Glen Urquhart. This leads up to some very beautiful country, the culmination of which is Glen Affric, whose deep, gorge-like loch scenery is enhanced by the coniferous trees that represent the remains of the ancient Caledonian Forest.

The south-east shore of Loch Ness has a motor road only from Foyers to Inverness. It follows the military road made by General Wade, which also continues along the edge of the lake to the south of Foyers and provides a good footpath for walkers. The motor road climbs inland up the Foyers River valley and then descends to Fort Augustus at the head of Loch Ness, where there is a splendid abbey built on the foundations of General Wade's Fort. There is an excellent Great Glen Exhibition in the town centre.

Loch Ness, famous for its monster, has a lovely wooded shore with handsome little villages. Urquhart castle, a splendid ruin built on a crag by the lakeside, was occupied by Edward I and blown up in 1692 to prevent the Jacobites using it.

The North-East Coast and the Grampians

On the whole, the longest rivers of Scotland are those that flow east, for, with the exception of the Grampians, the highest land in Scotland lies to the west. Beginning amid rocky gullies and bare mountain-sides, they flow through wooded glens, arriving eventually at broad valleys where they flow briskly past woods and pastures to the sea, their waters teeming with spawning salmon.

This gives immense variety to the eastern side of Scotland from Bettyhill, on the northern coast midway between Cape Wrath and John o' Groats, to Stirling, at the head of the Firth of Forth.

In the north the valleys, with their streams tumbling over stony beds, were once dotted with the houses of crofters, but they are almost empty now, and here and there a ruined cottage sits in its once-cultivated patch of greenery. Strathnaver, which was almost depopulated during the Highland Clearances in the nineteenth century, is a good example. Flowing from Loch Naver by the lonely village of Altnaharra in the midst of the open valley under Ben Klibreck, the River Naver runs through small pinewoods down to the north coast at Bettyhill. Despite its lack of dramatic features, it is a beautiful valley with expansive views all round, stretching, it seems, almost to infinity.

Farther east, in Caithness, low undulating land continues. The railway from Inverness runs across here on its way to Wick, from where a bus runs to John o' Groats. A short walk from this famous village gives visitors a breathtaking and memorable view, but not of the farthest northern point of the British mainland, for that is at Dunnet Head to the west, a few miles beyond the Queen Mother's castle at Mey.

Wick, where the railway line ends, was a Norse settlement and is now a royal burgh. It has a large harbour where the fishing boats congregate, and an airport from which there are flights to the Orkneys and the Shetlands. To the south of Wick stands all that remains of the castle of Old Wick, sometimes called Castle Oliphant, whose square ruined tower on a cliff top has been a landmark for sailors for centuries.

The cliffs are high and steep along the coast, and the restless North Sea is forever plucking and hammering at the rocks, gradually wearing clefts between the cliffs and forcing fishermen to drag their boats on to rock ledges away from the waves' destructive fingers. The coast is lined with tiny villages on this bleak north-east side of Scotland, some perched on clifftops, others clinging precariously to steep slopes. Lybster is one of these, with a steep lane down to a small rocky harbour where boats shelter; the strangely named Latheron Wheel is another, built on the edge of a wooded valley with a charming harbour below. At Dunbeath, built along a river valley that opens out into a bay, there are stone cottages and nearby to the south a castle rebuilt in the nineteenth century. It is not open to the public. At Helmsdale the village lies between green hills, and its port, where lobster fishermen congregate, is busy when the boats come in. Farther down the coast is Dunrobin Castle, ancient seat of the Dukes of Sutherland, which is now a school, and beyond a small sea loch named Fleet where there is a nature reserve and a ruined castle.

Dornoch stands at the wide entrance to the Dornoch Firth, the first real break in the coast all the way south from Wick. The Firth is surrounded by high hills from which there are fine views, especially from the road leading south to the Cromarty Firth. At the head of the Firth is Bonar Bridge, a small village where salmon fishermen gather to net the salmon in the Kyle of Sutherland upstream from the bridge.

Up the valley the castle of Invershin, called the Castle of Spite by local people because of the hatred of the Sutherland family for the unfaithful wife of the duke who inherited it on his, some say mysterious, death. This is a pretty glen, with trees along the slopes bordering the fishing stream which descends from Loch Shin, the largest loch in the central Highlands. At its southern end nestles the attractive village of Lairg, which has several hotels and caters for visitors passing through to the wild country to the north.

To the south, between the Shin Valley and the Strathconan Forest, lie the great mountain masses of Easter Ross, which are traversed by only two roads,

The pretty Shin Valley runs from Loch Shin southwards to Bonar Bridge and the Dornoch Firth. Near the Shin Falls at Invershin stands an impressive castle, called locally the Castle of Spite because, it is said, it was lived in by the unfaithful widow of the Duke of Sutherland, whose family refused to have any dealings with her.

Preceding page: Duncansby Head juts out to sea at John o' Groats providing views across the Pentland Firth to Orkney. Legend has it that John de Groot, a Dutchman, built the first house in the village, and the spot is marked today by a flagstaff. Contrary to popular belief, this is not the most northerly point of Britain's mainland, which is at Dunnet Head, some miles to the west.

one of which forks westwards at Invershin along Strath Oykel and the other along the southern edge of the mountains and following Dirrie More, passing Loch Glascarnoch. Both roads meet again at Ullapool on Loch Broom on the west coast.

The land tucked around the Dornoch, Cromarty and Moray Firths is fertile, and farmlands flourish, especially on the Black Isle peninsula south of the Cromarty Firth. The village of Cromarty, on the tip of the peninsula, is a cheerful place, with narrow winding streets and bright houses, and at Fortrose, on the southern shore, the remains of a cathedral built by David I of Scotland lies below the wooded hills.

Tucked away south of the Black Isle, where the Moray Firth meets the Beauly Firth which joins it from the west, is Inverness, the capital of the Highlands. This handsome old town is a busy shopping centre for almost all the Highlands and in summer is usually full of visitors heading north and seeking the advice of the Highlands and Islands Tourist Board office. The centre of the town is the Victorian town hall, near which lies the eighteenth-century castle and the museum. The original castle in which Macbeth may have murdered Duncan in 1039 no longer stands, and a later castle on the site was blown up by Bonnie

Prince Charlie in 1745. Further damage to the town was inflicted by the Duke of Cumberland after the battle of Culloden the following year. Inverness guards the eastern entrance to the Great Glen and is the exit point for the River Ness and the Caledonian Canal.

To the east of Inverness lies Culloden, today a small empty moor with only a cairn to commemorate the dead who fell in the great battle, and single stones to represent the clans that fought for the Young Pretender. There is a National Trust for Scotland audio-visual centre here, which recounts the story of the battle at which the Stuart dream died. Culloden House, nearby on the site of the original house used by Bonnie Prince Charlie as his headquarters, was rebuilt in the Adam style in the 1780s.

On the coast 16 miles (26 km) east of Inverness is the well-ordered and wooded town of Nairn, a golfing centre and site of Highland Games every August. There are several good hotels at this resort, whose attractions include sandy beaches and an interesting local history. The castle of Cawdor, a great dark square building amid trees 4 miles (6 km) south of Nairn, was built in the fourteenth century and so cannot offer any real connection with Macbeth, Thane of Cawdor. However, Rait Castle, also near Nairn, in which the Comyn Clan

Reflected in the waters of Loch Moy reservoir, in the Lochaber district, the 3,443-foot (1049-m) summit of Geal Charn is one of many high mountain peaks in this rugged part of the western Grampians. At the south-west end of the loch is a dam 180 feet (55 m) high and 700 feet (213 m) long.

were slaughtered by the Mackintoshes, whom they had invited into the castle as intended victims, is the original building in which the massacre took place in 1442, and its overgrown walls have a sinister air.

Elgin, a royal burgh with a famous ruined thirteenth-century cathedral, lies inland. The town was burned down by the Wolf of Badenoch in 1390 because the Bishop of Moray had reprimanded him for deserting his wife. Farther east along the coast is the mouth of the great River Spey which, after its magnificent journey from a watershed above the eastern end of the Great Glen, arrives at the sea almost unnoticed except by a few cottages at Kingston, once a shipbuilding centre but now almost uninhabited. The river, famous the world over for its salmon fishing, for which the town of Grantown-on-Spey is a centre, is the finest of the many lovely rivers that flow through this part of Scotland. Rising in Little Loch Spey within sight of Ben Nevis, it curves round the Monadhliath Mountains into a broad green valley bordered on the south-east by the Cairngorm Mountains. Along its route it passes Kingussie, where the gaunt ruins of the Ruthven barracks stand starkly on high ground on the right bank of the river. These were rebuilt in 1745 to house English soldiers, but before that a castle of the fearsome Wolf of Badenoch, Alexander Stewart, son of Robert II, stood here. Kingussie has a Highland Museum, which contains an interesting collection of items of daily life in the Highlands. An original castle of the Wolf, now in ruins, can be seen at Lochindorb at the northern end of the Spey valley.

Off the main road to the east of Kingussie lies Loch an Eilean, a small loch with an island on which stands a ruined castle. Here one can see the remains of what was once the Great Caledonian Forest, the trees providing shelter for deer, squirrels, foxes, wildcats and many species of wildfowl.

Aviemore lies a little to the north astride the main road. This complex of hotels, shops, and places of entertainment was built specially to develop Cairngorm tourism, both summer and winter, and it has succeeded. In summer it attracts visitors who want to enjoy the countryside of the Cairngorms and the many sporting facilities available, and in winter it is a winter sports centre with easy access, by a specially built road, to the mountain slopes.

Among the places of special interest in the vicinity the Glen More Forest Park stands out. Although treeless except on its lower slopes (the word 'forest'

Above: The Grampian Mountains stretch right across the southern Highlands, forming a rugged backcloth behind Loch Tulla. Here the road from Bridge of Orchy to Glen Coe crosses the wild stretch of country called Rannoch Moor.

Left: Elgin Cathedral was built in the thirteenth century and was damaged by the Wolf of Badenoch, the illegitimate son of Robert II, even before it was finished. It was wrecked again by Cromwell's troops in 1650, but enough remains to make it one of the most impressive ruins in Scotland.

signified a hunting preserve rather than woodlands), this is an area of great beauty with superb views and plentiful wildlife, and rises to the summit of Cairngorm at 4,084 feet (1 245 m).

The coast from the mouth of the Spey round to Aberdeen has many small picturesque fishing villages, such as Burghead, home of the Outward Bound Moray Sea School and near Gordonstoun School, which the Prince of Wales and his father attended. At Buchan Ness, Scotland's most easterly point, the coast runs north and south. Nearby, the busy seaport of Peterhead, on the River Ugie, is the main harbour for ships seeking protection from the pounding of the North Sea. Ten miles (16 km) upstream at Old Deer is Deer Abbey, a ruined Cistercian monastery situated on a lovely stretch of the river.

The flat lands of Buchan, whose green cattle pastures once tempted raiders from the mountains, give way to hilly country as one approaches Aberdeen, the granite-built third largest city in Scotland. Among Aberdeen's historical buildings are the fourteenth-century St. Machar's Cathedral, the church of St. Nicholas, the sixteenth-century Provost Ross's house and the Old Tolbooth. Until recently, fishing was a major part of the city's wealth, but today, as the capital city of the offshore oilfields, Aberdeen has a new source of prosperity. The city lies at the mouths of two great fishing rivers, the Dee and the Don, and inland there are scores of castles built to guard the rich lands of the two rivers against marauders.

Kildrummy Castle, once a seat of the powerful Earl of Mar and now a ruin amid attractive gardens, guarded the upper reaches of the Don, and nearby Craigievar, a tall, pink and elegant-looking castle with turrets, gables, conical roofs and a tower, stands over a tributary, the Leochel Burn. The Dee is even more liberally endowed with ancient fortresses, many of them in ruins but a few still well maintained. Among these is Aboyne Castle, whose 500-year-old building is now the home of the Marquess of Huntly. Abergeldie is another typically

Scottish castle standing by the Dee on the fringe of the grounds of Balmoral.

This royal estate was bought by Queen Victoria and Prince Albert in 1853 and rebuilt in the Victorian baronial style that one sees today. The castle itself is not open to the public, but the gardens are when the Royal Family are not in residence. Behind the castle rises the mountain of Lochnagar (3,786 feet/1154 m), which inspired Prince Charles's children's book *The Old Man of Lochnagar*. Across the river lies Crathie Church, whose services are attended by the Royal Family when they are at Balmoral.

Upriver lies Braemar in a beautiful, wooded valley and surrounded by heather-covered hills. There is another splendid castle at Braemar, overlooking the River Dee. Built by the 2nd Earl of Mar in 1628, it was burnt down later by the Jacobites and rebuilt in the eighteenth century. Braemar is popular with holidaymakers during the summer months, and when the Royal Highland Games take place in September it is difficult to find accommodation.

South of Aberdeen lies the coast of Kincardineshire and Angus, where tall cliffs and wide bays alternate. Stonehaven is a fishing village and holiday resort and has a whisky distillery in which the Prince Regent once had a share. To the south of Stonehaven is Dunnottar Castle, built on a huge rock with sheer cliffs all round it. This is an impressive site, and its ruined walls seem to echo the stone stacks which rise out of the sea round it. Another coastal stronghold stands

on the cliffs north of St. Cyrus. This is the Kaim of Mathers, built in the fifteenth century by a Barclay. In St. Cyrus Bay itself there is a nature reserve, where seals and wild sea birds can be seen.

The Marquis of Montrose, the famous Scottish leader whose military genius defied the English but who was eventually betrayed by a MacLeod of Assynt and hanged in Edinburgh in 1650, was born at Montrose at the mouth of the River Esk, which rises in the mountains to the south of Lochnagar. The town has preserved much of its old atmosphere and has winding streets and gabled houses, over which rises a 220-foot (67-m) steeple, from which the bell 'Big Peter' rings a curfew every night at 10. Montrose harbour has always been full of fishing and coastal vessels and now to these are added boats that service the North Sea oil rigs.

Arbroath, where the coast turns westwards up the Firth of Tay, is famous for its 'smokies', haddock smoked over oak fires. Trawlers line the quaysides of

Above left: Aberdeen has several times played a part in Scottish history from the time of Robert the Bruce to that of Bonnie Prince Charlie. More recently, this splendid granite city has become a centre of the North Sea oil industry as well as a major seaside resort.

Arbroath harbour, and the town possesses a ruined abbey in which Robert the Bruce signed Scotland's Declaration of Independence in 1320. King William the Lion is buried in the abbey, which was used as a hiding place for the Scottish Coronation Stone when it was taken from Westminster Abbey in London by Scottish Nationalists in 1951.

The Tay estuary runs far inland past the city and seaport of Dundee on its north bank. Dundee has been a royal burgh since the twelfth century and was long a centre of resistance to the English. There is not much left of the old walled town except the gate at Cowgate Port, since much of the town was rebuilt in the nineteenth century. In its centre there is an attractive old graveyard called the Howff, originally the meeting-place (or howff) of medieval guilds and then the orchard of a Franciscan monastery, the land of which was given to the town by Mary Queen of Scots. An amusing legend recounts how one of the

The old Bridge of Dee lies downriver from Braemar amid wooded hills, through which the River Dee cascades over rocky falls. The bridge has not been used since Prince Albert ordered a new one to be built during one of his frequent visits to Balmoral with Queen Victoria.

Overleaf: Glamis Castle has a long and lurid history including the murder of Malcolm II and the burning of Lady Glamis for witchcraft. Since the seventeenth century, when it acquired its present appearance, it has been a gracious home of the Earls of Strathmore and Kinghorne and of the Queen Mother.

comfortable houses round the graveyard was taken over by the ghosts of the graveyard, until its owner married a lass who set to work spring-cleaning it in a typically vigorous Scottish manner and drove the ghosts or 'bogles' out.

One of the dominant features of the town is the fifteenth-century Old Steeple, which rises above three parish churches sheltering together under one roof. The town is well supplied with open spaces, such as Balgay Hill and Dudhope Park, in which is Dudhope Castle once owned in the late seventeenth century by 'Bonnie Dundee', Graham of Claverhouse. Today Dundee devotes itself to industry, and the shipyards that built ships for explorers from the time of Franklin to Scott and Shackleton are still working. So, too, are the jam factories, which have been at work since the late eighteenth century, when Mrs. Keiller first began selling her delicious Dundee marmalade.

Inland from Dundee lies the fertile region of the Vale of Strathmore, in which lies Glamis Castle, home of the Earls of Strathmore. The fourteenth-century castle, which was rebuilt in a more French style in the seventeenth century, is said to be haunted, although visitors are unlikely to see any supernatural beings among the fine furnishings and armour decorating the interior. The Queen Mother spent much of her childhood here and Princess Margaret was born in the castle.

At the head of the Firth of Tay lies the lovely city of Perth on the River Tay. Perth was the capital of Scotland until 1437, when James I of Scotland was murdered here and the capital was moved to Edinburgh. The only remaining building of that period is St. John's Kirk, whose spire rises above the buildings in the centre of the town. It was here that John Knox began his campaign in favour of the Reformation and that the first destruction of Catholic churches began in Scotland.

Open spaces called the North and the South Inch extend along the west bank of the river on each side of the centre of the town. Bonnie Prince Charles used North Inch for training his troops in 1745, and near Perth Bridge stands the house of Catherine Glover, the Fair Maid of Perth of Sir Walter Scott's novel. Another writer associated with Perth is John Buchan, Lord Tweedsmuir, who was born in York Place.

Around Perth there are some famous castles. Huntingtower, to the west, played a strange part in history when it was used by the Earl of Gowrie as the place to keep James VI a prisoner. Scone Castle, nearby to the north of Perth, was the coronation place of Scottish kings. It was Edward I who first took the Coronation Stone to London, where it was and still is kept in Westminster Abbey under the Coronation Chair.

From Perth some splendid river valleys fan out to north and east. The River Tay has its source far inland in a most beautiful area of the southern Highlands at Loch Tay. The river flows east and then turns south near Ballinluig, where it is joined by the River Tummel from the north. This is a scenically superbly beautiful area, with the River Tummel flowing down through Pitlochry from Loch Rannoch and Loch Tummel, whose wonderful views were much enjoyed by Queen Victoria. Her favourite viewpoint, looking west to Rannoch and including the peak of Schiehallion (3,547 feet/1081 m), is still known as the Queen's View.

North of Pitlochry, famed for its drama festival, the valley closes in on the wooded gorge of Killiecrankie, where Bonnie Dundee, Graham of Claverhouse, was killed in a skirmish with the English. This is a most atmospheric place, carefully maintained by the National Trust for Scotland. On the north side of Killiecrankie the country opens up in a broad green valley, in which the River Garry, a tributary of the Tummel, flows. Blair Atholl and its splendid castle are situated here. The fairy-tale appearance of this fortress, given to it in the nineteenth century, softens the harder aspect of the thirteenth-century structure beneath. There are some fine tapestries in the castle as well as a collection of armour.

Between Pitlochry and Perth is Dunkeld, with its cathedral. The town lies in a wooded valley just off the main road and has great charm. Steep, wooded hills rise behind it and there are nature trails to follow among the trees. Opposite the town is Birnam Hill, standing at the entrance to Strath Bran, which is said to have been dug out by Bran, the hound of the great hunter Fingal.

The peak of Schiehallion dominates the western end of lovely Loch Tummel and forms the backdrop to Queen Victoria's favourite view of the lake, which is commemorated at Queen's View. West of Schiehallion lies Loch Rannoch.

Preceding pages: South-east of the handsome city of Perth, the River Tay meanders through a broad green valley above which rises Kinnoull Hill, a popular viewpoint. Elcho Castle lies nearby on the south bank.

The great system of rivers which flows towards Perth makes the south-eastern corner of the Highlands a region of a particular beauty: more intimate than the great open landscapes of the western Highlands and full of history, for this was a front line in the bitter wars against the English. For today's visitor they are endlessly fascinating and easy of access.

The North-West Highlands and the Hebrides

The west coast of Scotland, once seen, leaves in the visitor an indelible impression and a strong desire to return. Here the world seems to hang on an edge between sea and sky, between dream and reality, the quick-changing weather allowing infinite views of moors and mountains or closing them into a mysterious world wreathed in mist and cloud, in which the monsters and mermaids that frequent the coast in legend seem as natural as the seals and sea birds that perch on its rocks in reality.

From earliest times the coast was a scene of struggle, first between the Norse seamen who sailed across the North Sea and the Scottish inhabitants, and later between the clans that guarded their family lands jealously and ruthlessly despatched their enemies, until English law and order was imposed on them.

The south-western part of the Highlands coast has been largely the lands of the Campbells who dominated it, though not all the outlying peninsulas and islands, between the Firths of Lorne and Clyde. The peninsula of Kintyre, for example, though it has a town called Campbeltown, was actually MacDonald country, and the Isle of Arran in the Firth of Clyde was the home of three clans, the Hamiltons, Fullartons and Mackinnons.

With its mountain scenery and its little glens, Arran is very much part of the Highlands and is a popular tourist destination in summer. The grandest parts of Arran lie to the north, where Goat Fell rises to 2,866 feet (874 m) and the port of Lochranza, where Robert the Bruce landed in 1306, is the only safe anchorage. On the east coast there are more harbours, and on one of them, Brodick, a castle guards the shore.

All the long peninsulas and islands of this fragmented part of Scotland were much-disputed territory, and the Campbells maintained a castle at Skipness at the entrance to Loch Fyne. The loch stretches northwards from Kintyre between the districts of Knapdale and Cowal to Inveraray, the main Campbell stronghold, which today is a much-visited town. Inveraray castle and town, headquarters of the Lords of Argyll, was rebuilt in the eighteenth century after being burnt down by the Scottish leader the Marquis of Montrose. The scenery around the white-walled town and castle is very fine, with wooded hills surrounding the loch and town. Rob Roy, the Scottish outlaw whose exploits were romanticized by Sir Walter Scott, lived in one of the glens nearby.

Running parallel to the Kintyre peninsula are three islands of the Inner Hebrides, Islay, Jura and Colonsay, reached by Steamers from Tarbet, which lies between Kintyre and Knapdale, or from Ardrossan on the Firth of Clyde. The islands are all very different in character. Jura is the most dramatic of the three, with rugged mountains which reach their maximum height (2,571 feet/784 m) at the Paps of Jura, while Islay is flatter, peat-covered, and has good beaches which attract summer visitors, who also enjoy the whisky for which Islay is renowned. Colonsay is the smallest of the three and has a rocky coastline and sandy beaches.

Glen Sannox is one of many pretty valleys on the Isle of Arran, a famous beauty spot in the Firth of Clyde. Mountains rise over 2,500 feet (762 m) in the north of the island, and most of the land consists of wild moors and fells. Along the coast are many small but popular summer resorts.

Overleaf: Kilchurn Castle stands on a flat promontory at the northern end of Loch Awe. Legend has it that it was built by the faithful wife of Sir Colin Campbell while he was away at the wars. The impressive scenery round the loch includes Ben Cruachan, in whose interior is a powerful hydro-electric station.

187

The islands lie at the southern extremity of the long trench which splits
mainland Scotland in two, the Great Glen. The southern entrance to this
geological fault, which by means of its lochs and the Caledonian Canal allows the
passage of ships between the west and east coasts of Scotland, is the Firth of
Lorne, lying between the mainland and the Isle of Mull.

Access to Mull is by ferry from Oban, an important port and harbour set in a
ring of hills, from which there are splendid views of the port's busy docks and of
the island of Kerrera, which defends its entrance. Oban is a fine Victorian town,
its skyline dominated by an amazing folly in the shape of the Colosseum in
Rome, which was built in the 1890s by a former resident of Oban named
McCaig. In its interior are public gardens, from which many a visitor takes
photos of the town framed by a neo-Roman arch.

The country surrounding Oban is rich in history and scenic splendour.
Immediately to the north along the coast lie the castles of Dunollie, from which
the MacDougalls, Lords of Lorne, controlled a large part of Scotland, and
Dunstaffnage, isolated on a grassy peninsula and surrounded by trees. This
splendid fifteenth-century fort was built as a base of operations against the
Norsemen, but its most dramatic moments took place with the murder of Sir
James Stewart during his wedding to his common-law wife in order to make
their son the legitimate heir to a kingdom coveted by the MacDougalls and the
Campbells.

Dunstaffnage stands near the entrance to Loch Etive, a beautiful loch whose
entrance is almost closed by a reef of rocks over which the ebbing tide falls in a
tumultous cascade called the Falls of Lora. From the falls there are roads on both
sides of the loch, to Bonawe quarries on the north bank and to Taynuilt on the
south. At Bonawe, one of the old iron-smelting furnaces which made cannons for
Nelson's ships has been preserved as a piece of industrial archaeology. There is
some wonderful scenery from Taynuilt. Loch Etive, where Deirdre of the
Sorrows, daughter of the king of the Picts, lived before her unwilling departure
for Ireland to marry the king of Ulster, is a lovely stretch of water which can
only be seen on foot or by boat. At its upper end are the mountains of Glen Coe.

South-east of Taynuilt the road goes through the Pass of Brander, whose steep,
scree and scrub-covered slopes make an impressive corridor to Loch Awe. Ben
Cruachan (3,695 feet/1 126 m) towers over the left bank; in a huge cavern inside
the mountain, created by one of the largest quarrying operations ever made in
Britain, is the Cruachan hydro-electric power station. The pass opens out into Loch
Awe and there is a fine view of the awesome ruins of Kilchurn Castle, built by the
wife of Colin Campbell of Glenorchy in the fifteenth century. Both sides of Loch
Awe are edged by roads as far as its south-western extremity. The northern road
takes one through the Inverliever Forest and the southern one through Eredine
Forest, making the choice of routes difficult for they are both beautiful.

To the north-east of the loch is another most enchanting valley, Glen Orchy,
down which the River Orchy foams and tumbles over the rocks where trout
fishermen stand casting flies on the pools below the cascades. Glen Orchy leads
up to Little Loch Tulla and Rannoch Moor. This desolate piece of moorland
between the head of Glen Coe and Loch Rannoch is a swampy area of peat bogs,
from which rivers run to the east and west coast of Scotland. Impressive for its
wild bleakness rather than its beauty, Rannoch Moor is crossed by a road and the
railway line to Fort William. From both there are superb views of the Glen Coe
mountains and the Marmore Forest.

Glen Coe is the showpiece of this austere and beautiful landscape, which
attracts sightseers in summer and skiers in winter, and as a setting for the dark
story of the massacre by Campbell soldiers of the MacDonalds of Glencoe in
1692, it could not be bettered. On its southern flank rise the massive rocky
heights of Buchaille Etive Mor, the great Herdsman of Etive, and the Three
Sisters, and on the north the heights of Aonach Eagach over which winds one of
the roads, called the Devil's Staircase, and now a track, made by General
Caulfield during the period of the pacification of Scotland after Bonnie Prince
Charlie's defeat.

The road down Glen Coe is exhilarating enough to drive through, but even
better is to walk along it or along the edge of the Coe stream, with the waterfalls

Ballachulish lies at the mouth of Loch Leven, the entrance to Glen Coe from the west. Beyond rise the Paps of Glencoe, on the slopes of which the MacDonalds died in the wintry cold as they fled from the treacherous Campbells.

that enter it from the surrounding mountains filling the air with the sound of rushing waters. There is a good National Trust for Scotland visitor centre near the Signal Rock from which the MacDonalds called their people in an emergency, and at the foot of the pass lies the village of Glencoe on the shores of Loch Leven. Where Loch Leven meets the sea loch, Loch Linnhe, the Ballachulish bridge carries the main road over the narrow waters. Fort William, the gateway to the Great Glen, lies at the head of Loch Linnhe. At its southern end, the loch opens out into the Atlantic Ocean, which washes the shores of the island of Mull.

Mull, whose indentations make it look like a map of Britain drawn by Gerald Scarfe, is an entrancing island with lovely scenery and a romantic history. At the very entrance to the Sound of Mull, north of the island, as the steamer from Oban wends its way to Craignure, Mull's main port, one sees Duart Castle on its lonely crag by the water's edge. It was originally built by the Lord of the Isles in the thirteenth century and subsequently passed to the Macleans, one of whose lords left his wife, a Campbell, to perish on an offshore rock, now called Lady Rock. She was, however, rescued, returning to her family, who eventually dealt with her unfeeling husband in the usual Highland manner.

At the northern end of the Sound of Mull is Tobermory, a port whose painted houses, fishing boats and colourful quaysides make everyone reach for their

camera. Off-shore, and buried deep in the mud of the harbour, lies the sunken wreck of the *Duque de Florencia*, an Armada galleon loaded, so it is said, with gold and jewels. From Tobermory, boat excursions can be made to the offshore islands of Coll and Tiree, and to Barra and South Uist in the Outer Hebrides.

The north of Mull is a wild and windswept coast, with seas breaking against rocks and cliffs; the west coast is more sheltered by islands, which feature prominently in the splendid views from the main island. In the centre of Mull, between Lochs Na Keal and Scridain, rises Ben More (3,169 feet/966 m), and south of it, along the southern side of Loch Scridain, is the road to the Ross of Mull, where is the embarkation point for Iona. This holy isle, on which St. Columba and his followers founded a monastery in 563, has an almost mesmeric quality, seeming to float between sky and sea. Less than a hundred people live on it now, but in summer thousands of visitors arrive on the ferry from Fionnphort or by steamer from Oban to visit the restored monastery (now the home of the Iona Community), the cathedral and St. Oran's chapel.

North of the Island of Mull extends the mainland peninsula of Ardnamurchan, the most westerly point of mainland Britain and whose name means 'Point of the Great Ocean'. There is only one secondary road along the edge of Loch Sunart, which borders it to the south as far as the open sea, and from the north shore of the peninsula one can see the quaintly named islands of Muck, Eigg and Rhum.

Above right: The railway viaduct across Glenfinnan, at the head of Loch Shiel, was built by Thomas Telford. Glenfinnan was the spot where Bonnie Prince Charlie raised his standard and summoned the clans to help him win the crown for his father. An excellent museum tells the sad story of his failure.

To the east of Ardnamurchan lies the southern end of Loch Shiel, much of which is accessible only on foot along a foresters' path. At its northern end is the road from Fort William to Mallaig. Here both road and railway pass by Glenfinnan, the spot where Bonnie Prince Charlie raised his standard and called on the clans to support him in his effort to win back the throne of Britain for his father, James III, the Old Pretender. To commemorate his brave but quixotic effort there is a monument by the lakeside, and there is also a National Trust for Scotland visitor centre where the whole sad story of Bonnie Prince Charlie is well told.

The Glenfinnan road leads eastwards to Fort William, which is a popular centre for excursions in this scenically rich area, dominated by the 4,406-foot (1343-m) summit of Ben Nevis. The highest mountain in Britain is not visible from the centre of Fort William but once in Glen Nevis it looms up at the end of the valley. The glen leads up through fields and trees, with a stream rushing past grassy slopes on which sheep graze, and then enters a gorge open to walkers only, where sheer cliffs 2,000 feet high (over 600 m) stretch for nearly two miles (3 km).

The only scenery comparable to that of Ben Nevis is on the Isle of Skye, reached by road or rail from Fort William via Mallaig on the North Morar

Peninsula or from the Kyle of Lochalsh, whose railway runs from Inverness on the east coast. Skye is perhaps the most romantic of the Inner Hebrides, with its wild scenery and its history first as a Viking headquarters and later as the battleground between MacLeods and MacDonalds.

From Kylekean, the crossing point on the Skye side, which is no more than half a mile (800 m) from the Kyle of Lochalsh on the mainland, a road leads up the northern side of Skye to the main town, Portree, and to the northern peninsulas of Trotternish, Vaternish and Duirnish. Between the latter two lies Dunvegan Loch and the Macleod castle of Dunvegan, in whose dungeon were imprisoned all those who tried to challenge the MacLeod power. According to legend, this power was derived from a flag given to the MacLeods by a fairy, who promised that it would bring them success in battle as long as it was used only three times. The flag is still shown to visitors to Dunvegan Castle, an impressive turreted building which towers over the loch and is today surrounded by a pleasant garden. Dunvegan is the oldest inhabited castle in Scotland, its occupancy going back 700 years.

The fragmented south-west coast of Skye includes the Minginish Peninsula, on which rise the Cuillin Hills, a mountaineer's paradise, but not exclusively, for a road skirts their northern edge to Glen Brittle and Glen Sligachan, easily walkable from Sligachan village. The road also gives access to Loch Coruisk, which is surrounded by the best of the Cuillin peaks.

The Outer Hebrides are only two hours away from Uig, on Skye's Trotternish Peninsula, and in summer the steamers are busy carrying visitors to and from this isolated part of Britain. The Long Island, as the Hebrides are known locally, is a wild and varied collection of islands stretching over 100 miles (160 km) and separated from the mainland by the channels of the Minch and Little Minch.

Lewis, the largest island, has its capital at Stornoway, a fishing port and centre of the Harris Tweed industry. The harbour is always full of fishing boats and, in summer, pleasure boats, which shelter in the curve of hills on one of which stands Stornoway Castle. To the north of Stornoway lies the Butt of Lewis, the most northerly point of the Hebrides, which is accessible by road. There is also a road from Stornoway to the south over the loch-filled lands to the Tarbert Isthmus, which leads to Harris and a totally different landscape. Here, instead of flat lands full of lochans (small lochs), there are mountains up to 2,000 feet (610 m) high.

Across the Sound of Harris, the land of North and South Uist and Barra is low-lying again and so covered with lochans that it is difficult to distinguish whether one is on land or water. There are many standing stones as evidence that early inhabitants did not find these watery islands too inhospitable, and Bonnie Prince Charlie also found shelter and protection here when he was hiding from the English, who had put a price on his head after Culloden.

The northern part of the Hebrides is almost on the same latitude as the north coast of Scotland and there is a direct steamer service from Stornoway to Ullapool on Loch Broom. To the west of North Uist are the solitary islands of St. Kilda whose last inhabitants left in 1930. Now they are a sea-bird reserve.

To the south of Loch Broom lies the magnificent scenery of Wester Ross, including the vast, rocky wilderness of Loch Torridon whose glen is flanked by the Liathach mountain and Beinn Eighe. This is mountaineers' country but no less enjoyable for motorists, who can approach from the south, making the exciting Applecross detour if they fancy the thrills of a road with a 1 in 4 gradient, or from the north via Kinlochewe at the eastern end of Loch Maree. This loch is heavily wooded on its south slopes and on its islands, which are mirrored in the loch's calm waters. On the north-east side the view includes Slioch rising majestically to 3,215 feet (980 m) and making the loch one of the finest in Scotland.

The western end of the loch fails to reach the sea by a couple of miles (around 3 km) but is joined to Loch Ewe, a sea loch, by the River Ewe. Loch Ewe is itself almost totally enclosed by land and is therefore sheltered from the wind, which is no doubt the reason why Osgood Mackenzie of the Gairoch clan chose it as the site for his remarkable Inverewe Gardens. The gardens were created in 1862 on a barren peninsula on the eastern shore of Loch Ewe and today are one

The church and cluster of houses that make up Glenfinnan lie along the road from Fort William to Mallaig, an embarcation point for the Isle of Mull ferry to Armadale. From Glenfinnan there are foresters' tracks, but no roads, along Loch Shiel, which runs south-west towards the sea.

Overleaf: Ben Nevis, at 4,406 feet (1343 m) the highest mountain in Britain, has a rugged north-east face and a gentle slope to the south which makes it easy to climb. The mountain towers above Inverlochy Castle, in the Great Glen some two miles (3 km) north of Fort William.

Above: Eilean Donan Castle stands on an island joined to the shore by a causeway in Loch Duich at the point where it becomes Loch Alsh. The scenery around it is spectacular and the castle itself, rebuilt after having been shelled by English ships in 1745, is one of the most interesting in the Highlands.

of the wonders of the Highlands, with their subtropical vegetation in latitudes that are more used to conifers and lichens than magnolias and rhododendrons. From spring, the best time to visit, to late summer many people come to walk here and admire the gardens, which stretch over some 2,000 acres (809 hectares) amid superb scenery.

Over the hill to the north of the gardens lies Gruinard Bay, an enchanting bay with sandy beaches; but beware, for the island in the centre of the bay was contaminated with anthrax in experiments conducted during World War II and it is still not safe, or permissible to visit. The next loch is Little Loch Broom, a perfect threshold to Loch Broom itself. An Teallach (3,484 feet/1 062 m) dominates the landscape and provides good walking country, with extensive views over Loch Broom and the mountains to the north.

Ullapool is strung along the northern shore of Loch Broom, with its white cottages facing the beach, on which fishing boats and sailing craft of all descriptions are moored. There is a big quay, where the steamers for Stornoway come alongside, and several good hotels. Up the loch the forests thicken, and among the trees is the Corrieshalloch gorge, with its waterfall, crossed by a narrow pedestrian bridge.

To the north of Ullapool lies a corner of the Highlands that seems like a kingdom on its own. there is only one road round it and most of it is single track with passing places, but it passes through some wonderful country fringing the kingdom within its boundaries. Here are incredible sugar-loaf mountains, rising sheer out of the loch-covered countryside rich in wildlife. On its southern edge by Loch Lurgainn is the Inverpolly Forest, with the shattered head of Stac

Below: The well-preserved little village of Plockton is situated on a peninsula at the mouth of Loch Carron in the lee of high hills. It is a popular place with artists, and behind it, to the south and the shores of Loch Alsh, stretch the wooded grounds of the Balmacara estate.

Above: The ghost of a girl whose lover was sealed into the castle walls haunts Ardvreck castle on Loch Assynt. This lonely ruin is in wild and desolate country near the Inchnadamph National Nature Reserve, where caves contain stalactites and where prehistoric animal bones have been found.

Above left: Harris is the southern half of the most northerly island of the Hebrides and is itself divided at the Tarbert Isthmus into North Harris and South Harris, where the rocky landscape is studded with small lochs. Genuine Harris Tweed cloth is still handwoven by the islanders.

Left: Fishing boats provide a lively spectacle at Ullapool where white cottages line the shores of Loch Broom. On the southern side of the loch rises Beinn Nam Ban (1,901/579 m), and at its head are the Measach Falls in the Corrieshalloch Gorge.

Polly rising to 2,000 feet (610 m); farther inland is 2,787-foot (849-m) Cul Mor, and north of that, across Loch Veyatie, are Suilven (2,399 feet/731 m) and Canisp (2,779 feet/847 m). None of them is big, as mountains go, but nevertheless their setting and outlines make them as impressive as mountains twice as high.

To the north across Loch Assynt, whose eastern end is marked by the romantic ruins of Ardvreck Castle, lies Quinag (2,654 feet/809 m), and to the east the Inchnadamph Forest, above which Ben More Assynt rises to 3,273 feet (998 m). These mountains and those to the north are the watershed from which the rivers of the east and west Highlands flow, the east-flowing ones having a longer journey to the sea than those to the west.

The landscape of the Highlands is at its most solitary in this north-east corner of Scotland, but its beauty is undiminished as summit follows summit. Arkle (2,580 feet/786 m), north of Loch Stack, Foinaven (2,980 feet/908 m) and Cranstackie (2,630 feet/802 m) form a mountain barrier, decreasing in height as it approaches Cape Wrath, between the north-west coast and the great plateau to the east, whose rivers empty into the Atlantic Ocean off the north of Scotland. Here Ben Hope (3,040 feet/927 m) and Ben Loyal (2,504 feet/763 m) stand out in solitary splendour.

As far as Bettyhill, named after the wife of the Duke of Sutherland, whose ill-advised clearances of the Highlands in order to introduce sheep rearing caused much suffering and emigration of crofters to Australia, Canada and New Zealand, the Highland character of the lochs continues. Loch Eriboll, in particular, is a magnificent sea loch, and the Kyle of Tongue, though much silted up since the ship bringing gold to help Bonnie Prince Charlie took refuge there, is a beautiful place with a fine village and the castle of the Mackays adding drama to its western slopes.

Inland is Altnaharra, at the foot of Ben Klibrick (3,154 feet/961 m), where the land begins its eastward slope and the streams head for the North Sea across a desolate and spacious countryside. Here purple heather flourishes in the summer, when a few peat diggers may be seen labouring at their trenches, and those with sharp eyes and field glasses may see the herds of deer. But in winter the land is under snow and the narrow road impassable much of the time.

The Orkneys and Shetlands

Off the north-east corner of Scotland lie the rugged archipelagoes of the Orkney and Shetland Islands, which are predominantly low-lying but with high cliffs and moorlands. They stretch north towards the Arctic Circle but are kept warm enough by the Gulf Stream to maintain a population of fishermen and farmers. The Orkneys are separated from the north-east mainland of Scotland by the Pentland Firth. They have a distinct character of their own, no doubt because they and the Shetlands were settled early on by the Norsemen, both groups of islands becoming Scottish only in 1468 on the marriage of the daughter of Christian I of Norway to James III of Scotland.

Kirkwall is the capital of the Orkneys and lies in the centre of Mainland, the largest of the group of 65 islands of the group. Its cathedral, founded in the twelfth century in memory of St. Magnus, has his bones buried in one of the church pillars. To the south of Kirkwall is Scapa Flow, a famous sheltered naval base where the German navy was held and scuttled 74 ships after World War I and where, during World War II, an audacious German submarine sank the Royal Navy's *Royal Oak*.

The Shetlands, lying some 50 miles (80 km) north of the Orkneys, number a hundred islands in the group, only about 15 of which are inhabited. The capital of the Shetlands is Lerwick, the most northerly town in Britain and a busy fishing port which handles the great catches from the islands' fleet of trawlers. To the north the land of Britain comes to an end at Muckle Flugga, over 170 miles (274 km) north of John o' Groats. Here a lighthouse blinks out its lonely message on a rocky island where sea birds thrive and the sea is still a rich fishing ground.

Between the two groups of islands lies tiny, remote Fair Isle, famous among ornithologists for the great number of species of bird which may be observed there and famous, too, for the intricate knitting patterns worked by the islanders.

Above: The Shetland Islands, though north of the Orkneys, are warmed by the Gulf Stream. Seventeen of the hundred islands are inhabited and many more receive summer visitors looking for tranquillity or attracted by the abundant bird life.

Right: The remains of a crofter's house at Rackwick Bay on Hoy, one of the Orkney Islands. There are about seventy islands in the Orkney archipelago, which has gradually become depopulated as the young drift away to jobs in mainland industries. Orkney people are of Norse ancestry and traces of it are evident in their speech, place names and local festivals.

Wales

Despite the various invasions and conquest by Anglo-Saxons, Romans, Normans, and English the spirit of Wales has remained Celtic, enriching the arts of song, music and drama and giving to British history some of its most complex and colourful characters, among them the poet Dylan Thomas, the statesman Lloyd George, the composer Vaughan Williams, and the inscrutable adventurer Lawrence of Arabia.

Wales is another country, a fact of which the traveller is aware as soon as he crosses the border into the green mountains of Brecon or the vales of Clwyd and Llangollen. This is a moody land, awesomely grim in bad weather, beautiful as Welsh singing when the sun shines. It is a land of massive castles – many, such as Aberystwyth, Flint, Beaumaris, Harlech, Conway and Caernarvon, built by the English King Edward I and his followers to keep the Welsh suppressed after defeating their leaders, the Llewellyns – a land also of wooded streams up which the trout run and where woodpeckers, dippers and kingfishers live. It is a land of ancient mountains, the oldest in Britain, with a coastline which faces the stormy waters of the Atlantic, which flow up St. George's Channel with the same stubbornness that its early inhabitants presented to the human enemy from the east.

Along the Coast

The Welsh coast faces the Bristol Channel and the Atlantic in the south, St. George's Channel and the Irish Sea to the west and the tranquil tidal waters of the Dee estuary in the north. This give it an enormous variety of character, from the rugged headlands of the south-west to the holiday-resort beaches of the north. The south-eastern corner of Wales is very much an industrial coast. Here the coalmining valleys of Glamorgan and Gwent enter the British Channel, and the quays of the ports are lined with colliers waiting to load the coal and iron which transformed the green landscape of the eighteenth century into the industrial scene of today. Not everywhere, though: Tredegar House, just outside Newport, retains the warm loveliness of its seventeenth-century brick construction. Inside, it is being carefully restored to provide an oasis of calm from an earlier age.

This part of Wales was always a land coveted by invaders; the Romans built forts here, the ruins of one of which can be seen at Caerleon, near Newport. They also had a settlement at Cardiff, the capital of Wales and its greatest port. Originally a fishing village, Cardiff grew in the nineteenth century as a coal-exporting port. Today it is a great city with broad streets and important Civic Centre buildings. Cardiff's castle is Norman, built less than 30 years after William of Normandy became King of England, but restored in the nineteenth century. There are other medieval fortresses at Caerphilly, inland from Cardiff and famous for its Caerphilly cheese, at Bridgend, and at Oystermouth near Swansea.

Oystermouth, with its neighbour The Mumbles, is on the Gower Peninsula just south of Swansea and provides a cheerful small seaside-town atmosphere for

The River Mawddach flows from the mountains of Gwynedd through Dolgellau and into an estuary which stretches down to Barmouth on Cardigan Bay. From the north bank of the estuary there are fine views of Cader Idris, which towers to 2,927 feet (891 m) to the south.

the industrial workers along the coast. One of the first railway lines in Britain was established here with horse-drawn trucks in 1807, and later switched to steam to provide transport when the craze for seaside holidays began early in Queen Victoria's reign.

The Gower Peninsula itself gives a taste of the beauties to come on the west-extending coast. Here there are sandy coves sheltered by pine-clad cliffs, and there are beautiful views of cliff and sea from the coast path. Pwlldu Bay is one of these; to its south lies the Gower's highest cliff, over 250 feet (76 m) high. At the western end of the Gower one looks across to the small island of Worms Head, which derives its name from the ancient word for dragon, found also in Scotland. A huge, sandy beach stretches northward.

Overleaf: Cardiff, the capital of Wales, has a spacious modern Civic Centre in Cathays Park, which adjoins Bute Park on the River Taff. The castle, rebuilt by the Marquis of Bute in the 1870s, is at the southern end of the park, and beyond it is the Welsh national rugby shrine, Cardiff Arms Park.

On the mainland north of the peninsula, the traveller enters an industrial landscape again at Llanelli, but farther west, beyond Carmarthen, where King Arthur's magician Merlin was born and where the ruins of the Norman castle still dominate the town, there comes a more rural scenery. Laugharne, on the western side of the Carmarthen estuary, is a pilgrimage spot for poets, because Dylan Thomas lived, worked and is buried here. Since the poet lived here for sixteen years, it is assumed that Laugharne was his model for *Under Milk Wood*.

Farther west, at the popular resort of Tenby, the coast rises with hills and cliffs, among which the picturesque walled town, with its neat white houses, looks like a stage set. Two and a half miles (4 km) offshore is Caldy Island, whose monks make perfumes in the priory.

The Pembroke Peninsula (south-west Dyfed) is famed as one of the most beautiful sections of the Welsh coast, and most of it is a National Park. This indented shore, with its cliffs and wave-washed headlands and cut by the long, sheltered Milford Haven estuary, has splendidly wild scenery, much of it skirted by one of the best-loved coastal walks in Britain, the Pembrokeshire Coastal Path. Oil tankers looking like toy ships ply up and down the Haven but, except round Milford Haven itself, one of Europe's major oil ports, do not spoil the views. The town of Pembroke, small, bustling and over-shadowed by the huge outlines of its well-preserved Norman castle, where Henry Tudor was born, rests on the banks of the Pembroke River, which flows into the south-eastern arm of Milford Haven estuary.

North of Milford Haven is St. Bride's Bay, a vast semicircular bay enclosed by two headlands, off which lie the islands of Skomer and Skokholm and to the north, Ramsey. On these islands lives abundant wildlife, especially sea birds and colonies of grey seals, which breed in the protected waters. On the northern arm of the peninsula lies St. David's, a small town classified as a city because of its lovely twelfth-century cathedral, named after the patron saint of Wales who was born here. The cathedral and the ruins of the medieval bishops' palace lie in a green hollow near the sea, where there are beaches, cliffs and small bays, one of which, St. Non's Bay, is claimed as the actual place of the saint's birth.

Rather surprisingly in view of the rocky nature of the coast, inland there is only a gentle slope over moorlands to the highest point at Mynydd Prescelly (1,760 feet/536 m), where the blue stones for Stonehenge were quarried. To the north of these hills lies Fishguard, a port for ferries to Ireland and an attractive town, much of it built on a hill above the port. The last armed invasion of Britain took place here, or more correctly at Goodwick next door, in 1797, when a force of Frenchmen landed but soon surrendered at a table still to be seen at the local Royal Oak pub.

The great northward sweep of Cardigan Bay lies between St. David's Head and the Lleyn Peninsula, which juts out from Snowdonia in the north of Wales. Along its southern stretch, in the country of Dyfed, lies one of the least-inhabited parts of Wales, where Welsh traditions survive strongly and the majority of the population speak the Welsh language. Farther north, where the coast approaches the county of Gwynedd, lies the attractive seaside town of Aberystwyth, seat of the University of Wales and the National Library, and with a history that can be traced back 6,000 years.

The sea front at Aberystwyth is lined with well-maintained Victorian and Edwardian houses, sweeping in an elegant parade round the promenade that ends at its southern extremity among the Victorian Gothic buildings of the University of Wales, established in 1860. At the northern end the land rises steeply to Constitution Hill, which can be reached by a cable railway. Behind the front the town rises up into the hills, through which runs the Afon Rheidol. There is a twelve-mile (19-km) excursion on a small-gauge steam railway up the valley to Devil's Bridge, a triple bridge across the River Mynach.

North of Aberystwyth the River Dovey flows into the sea in a broad estuary which cuts into the smooth outline of the coast. At its head lies the fine town of Machynlleth and on the northern bank at the mouth is Aberdovey, a port and resort with sandy beaches. A local legend says that much of the land here sank below the waves and that the bells of the sunken churches can be heard tolling when danger threatens the town. From Tywyn, along the coast, there is another

Laugharne Castle dominates the estuary of the Taff and Tywi rivers, on Carmarthen Bay in South Wales. Laugharne is best known as the home of Dylan Thomas, the poet, who lived at Boat House by the shore close to the castle.

of Wales' famous steam railways, this one built in 1865 and running up the valley to Abergynolwyn.

The Mawddach estuary to the north is in Snowdonia National Park, which makes its entry here in a dramatic way, with Cader Idris rising 2,927 feet (892 m) to the south. This view led John Ruskin to exclaim that the walk from Dolgellau at the head of the estuary to Barmouth at its mouth was only exceeded in beauty by the walk in the opposite direction. The sands along the stretch of coast north of Barmouth make it popular with summer visitors, but there are few resorts, for the land is low-lying and marshy, rising suddenly and dramatically at Harlech. Here the great castle built by Edward I was the scene of the capture of the family of Owen Glendower, the Welsh resistance leader, by Henry V.

Tucked away in the corner of Tremadoc Bay, where the Welsh coastline curves westward along the Lleyn Peninsula, is the Dwyryd estuary, where the Italianate dream of architect Clough Williams-Ellis became a reality. Portmeirion is an unlikely village in which romantic Italian facades, terraces, columns, piazzas, and a campanile emerge from palm trees, rhododendrons and mimosa to recreate the atmosphere of the Ligurian coast in a Welsh landscape. The effect of this fantasy is enchanting and, though blue skies help to enhance the illusion, even on winter days Williams-Ellis' creation lightens the heart.

The wild peninsula of Strumble Head lies between St. David's, whose cathedral is the Canterbury of Wales, and Fishguard, an embarkation point for ferries to Ireland.

Left: The white cottages of Borth, north of Aberystwyth, are strung out along the shore of Cardigan Bay. Behind the attractive village rise the mountains, and to the south is Upper Borth, from which there are splendid views of the coast.

Near Portmeirion are two other interesting old towns, Tremadoc and Portmadoc, both on the mouth of the Glaslyn River, which flows down from Snowdon. The towns were the work of a nineteenth-century Member of Parliament, William Alexander Maddocks, who reclaimed the land from the estuary and encouraged the building of what he aspired to make the model town of Tremadoc. T. E. Lawrence was born here and may have indulged his love of adventure on the cliffs behind the town on which young mountain climbers try their skills today. Portmadoc, by the estuary, was once lived in by the poet Shelley, who was shot at while staying there and left hurriedly. Today it is a busy little harbour filled with small craft.

The Lleyn Peninsula, which stretches westwards, continues the ruggedness of Snowdonia with steep, rocky cliffs and craggy summits that rise above the green farmlands. This wild, windswept area was much inhabited by early missionaries from Ireland, and Bardsey Island off the extreme western end was reputed to be the burial place of saints and holy men.

Above: The Rhinog mountains rise behind the Artro estuary, which heads inland from Llanbedr on the west coast of Wales between Barmouth and Harlech. At the upper end of the valley is Pen-y-Bont, from which there is an easy ascent of the Rhinogs.

Overleaf: The Italianate village built by Clough Williams-Ellis at Portmeirion is one of the most successful follies of the twentieth century. The gardens are planted with subtropical plants, which strengthen the illusion of a Mediterranean town.

Pwllheli, on the south coast, is the most popular resort of this area. It has an old town as well as a modern resort, whose harbour is much used by pleasure craft. Criccieth, to the east, was the birthplace of Britain's charismatic Prime Minister, Lloyd George. Its castle was built, not by Edward I, but by the Welsh, though it later fell into the English king's grasp.

The north coast of the Lleyn Peninsula is exposed to the west winds and the battering of the Irish Sea. From the hills above Tre'r Ceiri there are wonderful views across the sea to Anglesey and, on a clear day to Ireland and the Isle of Man.

Anglesey dominates this part of the Welsh coast. Once a granary for the mainland, it is now a rugged land of small-holdings, among which are found stone relics of the Neolithic and Bronze Ages. At its farthest western edge is Holyhead, the railhead and embarkation point for Ireland. Steep cliffs and mountains rear up above the sea here, and Holyhead Mountain, though only 720 feet (219 m) high, gives spectacular views. The island is joined to the mainland at Bangor by a road and a rail bridge over the Menai Strait, the former built by Thomas Telford and the latter by Robert Stephenson.

In medieval times, this was an embattled part of Wales, with Edward I blockading Anglesey to prevent the movement of supplies from the island and later building castles to maintain his hold over the country. Caernarvon was one of these. Built on a rock, with the town clustering around one side of it and the sea on the other, the castle, where Edward created the first Prince of Wales in 1301 and Prince Charles was invested in 1969, still has a formidable look. A wall runs round the old town, which has narrow streets and medieval buildings, many of them now shops for the thousands of tourists who come here every year. Proof of the importance of the link with Anglesey lies in the presence of the Roman fort of Segontium not far away to the south-east.

Edward also built a castle on the Anglesey side of the straits at Beaumaris. This fine example of a medieval fortress is still in a good state of preservation and, with its attractive town, makes a pleasant place for a visit.

Left: The Menai Bridge, which carries road traffic over the Menai Strait between Wales and Anglesey, was built by Thomas Telford in 1826. This is the only road connection with the island, but there is also a railway bridge built by Robert Stephenson in 1850.

The mountains of Snowdonia's northern edge border the sea between Bangor and Great Ormes Head, the last stretch of the hilly coastline before the flat shores of the River Dee take over. The great resort of Llandudno lies on the landward side of the headland of Great Ormes Head, with Conway Castle dominating the landscape at the exit of the Conway River. The castle is well preserved and played its part in the domination of Wales and later in the Wars of the Roses, which ended when Henry Tudor, a Welshman, defeated Richard III and became King Henry VII. A little farther east, on Penrhyn Bay, is the popular resort of Colwyn Bay.

In strong contrast to the stony might of Conway, are the gentle glories of Bodnant, a short drive south of Conway Castle in the Conway valley. This vast National Trust garden is famed for its luxuriant plantings of camellias, magnolias, azaleas and rhododendrons. Views of Snowdonia from Bodnant are also memorable.

Beyond Colwyn Bay there are various resorts which provide holiday accommodation within reach of beach and Snowdonia. Together they make a fine pleasure ground for the great industrial cities of northern England.

Once Caernarvon Castle controlled the south-western entrance to the Menai Strait and the passage to Anglesey. Today the well-preserved castle is the setting for great ceremonial occasions and an attraction for visitors to Snowdonia.

Snowdonia and the Mountains of North Wales

Although Snowdonia is the area around Mount Snowdon, the Snowdonia National Park stretches from Cader Idris in mid Wales north to the Conway estuary and includes the wild country around Lake Bala. This is one of the most beautiful places in Britain, with rugged peaks, precipitous cliffs, small lakes, green valleys and a character that is decidedly Welsh. Snowdon is the centre of attraction both for sightseers and mountaineers, and the 3,560-foot (1,085-m) mountain can be both welcoming and challenging. From Llanberis there is even a railway for those either unwilling or unable to attempt the summit on foot. Llanberis is also the point from which the easiest ascent of Snowdon for walkers begins.

Leaving the village by road, one ascends the Llanberis Pass to Pen-y-Gwryd, where the Everest team stayed while practising for the first successful assault on

At 3,560 feet (1085 m) Snowdon is not a big mountain but it has a commanding presence. A railway transports those who are not prepared to walk up one of the paths which start from Llanberis or Beddgelert.

Everest in 1953. To the right the road runs to Beddgelert, which lies at the foot of Snowdon's southern face. This pretty village is renowned for the legend of Gelert, the hound of Llewellyn the Great, who was killed by his master when he mistakenly thought that the blood on the dog's jaws was that of his missing son. As it turned out, it was the blood of a wolf killed by Gelert as it attacked the child, who was found safely in some bushes. True or false, the legend attracts many visitors who believe it and arrive at the village to visit the dog's grave.

Legends thrive in this part of Wales, which is hardly surprising, for the Celtic strain is strong and the landscape lends itself to thoughts about the supernatural. From Beddgelert there is a good walk up the Aberglaslyn Pass, from which there are good views of the Glaslyn stream, which flows down from the slopes of Snowdon to the sea at Portmadoc.

Taking the road north from Peny-y-Gwryd, one reaches Capel Curig, which is well known for its Plas y Brenin activity centre, where all kinds of outdoor pursuits and the necessary tuition are available. Trout fishing on Lake Mymbyr and rock climbing on Snowdon are among the popular activities.

To the east of Capel Curig are the Swallow Falls, a lovely wooded spot where the Llugwy River divides in cascades which tumble over the rocks. The river joins the Conway at Betws-y-Coed, just below the stretch of valley known as the Fairy Glen because of the picturesqueness of the trees and undergrowth that hang over the river where it leaps and sparkles over rocks at the Conway Falls. The River Conway flows north from this wooded valley into a broader vale, passing under the old three-arch stone bridge at Llanrwst and so to Conway Castle on the north coast of Wales.

To the south of the Snowdon massif, past the slate quarries of Blaenau Ffestiniog and beyond the pretty Ffestiniog valley, up which travels a narrow-gauge railway, lies another range of mountains, the largest of which is Cader Idris near the town of Dolgellau.

Dolgellau is an old town which has been the gathering place for farmers and quarry workers from all the surrounding valleys for centuries. Today it is also a holiday centre for those who go to Wales every summer to enjoy its wonderful mountain scenery. The River Mawddach, which rises in the Cader range, runs through the town and under the seventeenth-century bridge. Owen Glendower, the Welsh patriot, held the last Welsh Parliament in Dolgellau; long before Glendower, the Romans had a camp at this junction of three of their roads. From Dolgellau one can enjoy the panoramic Precipice Walk along a path cut round the Moel Cynwch mountain and the similarly enjoyable but less breath-stopping Torrent Walk along the edge of the Clywedog stream. A more challenging walk is the ascent, by the Pony Walk, of Cader Idris itself.

The summit of the ten-mile-long range of mountains overshadowing Dolgellau rises to 2,927 feet (892 m), and from it there are magnificent views to the west

Llyn Dinas lies along the road between Beddgelert and Pen-y-Gwryd to the east of Snowdon. Llyn is the Welsh name for lake, a not uncommon feature of the landscape, especially in Snowdonia.

across the Irish Sea and to the east towards England. The walls of the south-east face are the remains of a volcanic cone surrounding the waters of Llyn Cau, in which a monster is said to reside.

From Dolgellau a valley leads north-east to Lake Bala (or Llyn Tegid), the largest natural lake in Wales. The present road follows the route of the old Roman road to their fort at Caer Gai at the south-west end of the lake. There are roads down both sides of Lake Bala and the views are splendid from both. The town of Bala, at the northern end of the lake, is a fishing and sailing centre.

Lake Bala is fed by the River Dee, which rises in hills to the south-west and leaves Bala to encircle the county of Clwyd, flowing first through the Vale of Llangollen and then north through that showpiece of English timbered houses, the city of Chester, where it enters its broad estuary on the Irish Sea.

The Vale of Llangollen is one of the beauty spots of Wales and inspired Browning and Kinglake, who both claimed that it was as memorable as any of the beautiful places that they had seen on their travels abroad. A magnet for many of the distinguished visitors to Llangollen in the nineteenth century was Plas Newydd (New Place), the home of two eccentric ladies who wore distinctly mannish clothes and numbered among their friends many of the famous people of the day. The house, which is a fine example of an eighteenth-century half-timbered mansion, can still be visited today.

The town of Langollen is usually a quiet place, except in July when the streets are filled with the sound of foreign voices and singing during the International Eisteddfod. This event, held appropriately in a land renowned for its singers and poets, is a great festival of folk traditions.

A mile and a half (2.4 km) from the town to the north-west are the ruins of the Valle Crucis Abbey, founded by Cistercian monks in the thirteenth century. It can be reached on foot or by boat, for it lies near the Llangollen Canal. This 46-mile-long (74-km) branch of the Shropshire Union Canal begins at the Horse-shoe Falls farther up the Dee Valley by Llantysilio church, whose seventh-century foundations are topped by twelfth-century walls and which contains some relics saved from Valle Crucis Abbey. The Llangollen Canal is one of the most popular

The cliffs of Cader Idris surround a lake, Llyn Cau, which, according to legend, is bottomless and harbours a monster. Dolgellau, to the north, is a popular starting point for a walk to the summit, which is four and a half miles away (7 km) by the shortest route.

on the whole English-Welsh canal network, and also one of the most spectacular, its engineering including the famous 126-feet-high (38-m) Pont-Cysyllte aqueduct over the Dee.

To the north of Llangollen lies the Clwydian range of mountains, which stretch northwards to the sea on the right bank of the River Clwyd. The river flows through a green and pleasant valley passing the once-fortified town of Ruthin, whose castle, built on older foundations, is itself a nineteenth-century creation. A reminder of its stirring history during the Wars of the Roses and the Cromwellian period is the curfew which is still rung every night at eight.

On the left bank of the Clwyd rise the hills of Denbigh. The town is perched on the side of a hill and is topped by a castle built by the Earl of Lincoln in the thirteenth century. The castle still has eight of its towers and considerable stretches of wall intact, and the views from it to the south-west are very fine. The explorer and journalist H. M. Stanley was born in Denbigh, though his cottage below the castle walls is no longer in existence.

As the Clwyd approaches the sea it passes St. Asaph, a small village with the smallest cathedral in Britain, which, founded in the sixth century, has been considerably restored. From here the Clwyd flows down to the sea at Rhyl, near the start of the dyke built by King Offa, which runs from north to south along the ancient borders of Wales.

Mid and South Wales

The great mass of the Black Mountains and the Brecon Beacons stretch across South Wales from the borders with Hereford to the River Tywi, on the east side of Dyfed county, and dominate the landscape. The mountains rise gently like some titanic sea swell up their grassy slopes to reach heights nearing 3,000 feet (or 900 m), often coming to an abrupt stop and diving dizzily down sharp inclines where screes of jagged rocks plummet to the green valleys below.

At the eastern end these bluffs overlook England and no doubt made splendid vantage points from which to watch out for advancing enemies. At Hay Bluff

The River Dee flows through the beautiful Vale of Llangollen, cascading over the Swallow Falls to the north and running under the Llangollen town bridge, one of the wonders of Wales. Llangollen is the setting for the International Music Eisteddfod every summer.

above the village of Hay-on-Wye, where bookshops are more common than grocers' shops and the village is usually full of book-lovers, there is a breath-stopping view downwards to the land crossed by Offa's Dyke, to the Black Mountains to the south, and to the Brecon Beacons to the south-west. The Beacons were places where fires were lit to warn of national danger, and from their summits it is easy to see why they were chosen. Along their southern edge runs the Talybont Forest, and the roads through the Taf Fechan and Taf Fawr valleys, which climb up to the Beacons from the mining valleys of Merthyr Tydfil, are among the most beautiful in South Wales.

To the west lies another part of the Black Mountains which, though here named in the singular, signifies a whole range, and the Brecon Beacons National Park. Huge grassy slopes rising to crags and cliffs are the characteristic of this beautiful region in which, where it descends to the Vale of Tywi, stands the great fortress-castle of Carreg-Cennen, given by the Welshman Henry Tudor to the man who helped him to gain the throne of England, Sir Rhys ap Thomas. Carreg-Cennen stands atop a sheer precipice, with fertile valleys stretching away in every direction.

Pistyll Rhaeadr is the highest waterfall in Wales, falling 240 feet (73 m) in two leaps, one of which drops a sheer 100 feet (30 m). Llanrhaeadr-ym-Mochnant, on the road between Oswestry and Lake Bala, is the nearest village.

Overleaf: The Sugar Loaf is one of the high hills that form a semicircle around Abergavenny Castle. The town of Abergavenny is on the River Usk, which runs through the Brecon Beacons National Park.

To the north of the Black Mountain and separated from it by the valley of the River Wye, are the main ranges of the Cambrian Mountains which form the spine of Wales. Here is an area of green valleys amid hills and mountains watered by the great rivers Wye and Severn, which rise in the Plynlimon Mountains of Central Wales. Along the Wye and its tributaries are the spas which attracted those who found a preoccupation with their health a convenient excuse for taking a holiday.

Landrindod Wells, on the River Ithon, a tributary of the Wye, was popular even in the time of Charles II and still receives visitors for spa treatments, though most people stay in Llandrindod Wells because it is an excellent centre from which to explore the Wye valley. Builth Wells, to the south, is on the Wye and, though it no longer functions as a spa, it is a holiday centre and in July the centre of the Royal Welsh Agricultural Show.

To the east of this area the hills rise to Radnor Forest which, like many other forests, was a hunting ground in medieval times and later, rather than a densely tree-filled region. The highest hill, The Smatcher, rises above New Radnor which, despite its name, is actually about 700 years old and possesses the ruins of a castle at least 200 years older still.

The River Severn, which rises near the source of the Wye, takes a northward curve through Wales before entering England and along its course are a number of pretty villages and towns. Llanidloes, which has a half-timbered market building in the centre of the town, is a rendezvous for people who are planning to set off up Plynlimon; Newtown is the centre of a sheep-rearing and agricultural area; and near Welshpool, which is almost on the English border, there are several castles which once guarded the frontier. Powys Castle, which dates back to the thirteenth century, is in an excellent state of preservation and has attractive and well-maintained formal gardens. Montgomery Castle, though a ruin, has a splendid situation overlooking the town, which has managed to preserve some fine half-timbered buildings.

Right: The Craig Goch dam retains the waters of one of the Elan Valley reservoirs, which are set amid lovely country in mid Wales. The nearest town to this unspoiled area is Rhayader and there is a road from here to the Caben Coch, Garreg-ddu, Penygarreg and Craig Goch reservoirs. The Claerwen reservoir, at the western end of the region, has a 184-foot (56-m) high dam.

The Neuadd Reservoir stretches out below the slopes of Pen y Fan, at 2,906 feet (886 m) the highest point of the Brecon Beacons. These treeless summits, where signal fires were once lit, have given their name to the National Park which includes the Black Mountains of south-east Dyfed.

Ireland

Ireland may be a small island but it manages to pack in an enormous variety of scenery and places of historical interest dating from Neolithic times to the present day. In the east the country is rich farmland, with here and there a range of hills like those of Wicklow; in the centre is a land of rivers and lakes; and in the west is the Ireland of wild rocky coasts and mountains, with some of the most romantic scenery of Europe.

The Industrial Revolution hardly touched Ireland, and the countryside has remained remarkably unspoiled and empty, while the absence of a machine-oriented civilization until quite recently has also preserved a leisurely way of life in which the imaginative Celtic temperament of the Irish people has had room to expand and to provide for visitors a view of life which is becoming rarer in the hustle and bustle of modern urban life.

The earliest evidence of man's presence in Ireland dates back to the last Ice Age, though evidence of some form of civilization goes back more than 3,000 to 4,000 years, when the first lake dweller settled in central Ireland. Stone circles, dolmens (burial chambers) and forts reveal that the land soon became well populated and that the people of the tribal communities continued their individual development well beyond the period when the rest of Europe was subjected to Roman influences. Left alone by the Romans, Ireland was less fortunate when the Vikings arrived and ravaged the land. Before this, the most

Left: The lakes of Killarney, in County Kerry, are Ireland's best-known beauty spot. There are three main lakes – Lough Leane, Lough Muckross and Upper Lough – all surrounded by richly forested slopes.

important early contribution to Irish culture was brought by Christian monks who settled in this new land and created many of the early monuments, towers, carved crosses and rudimentary stone buildings that fascinate visitors today.

The Irish monasteries were a seed-bed for the spread of Christianity throughout the British Isles, complementing the work of St. Augustine in south-east England. That Christian monks were at work as early as the ninth century is evident from remaining buildings at Monasterboice, near Drogheda in County Louth, at Inishmurray Island in County Sligo and the minute church on St. MacDara's Island, County Galway.

The next great age of building did not come until the eighteenth century, following the defeat of James II by William III at the Battle of the Boyne in 1690. This brought about the period of the Protestant Ascendancy, during which castles and manor houses sprang up throughout Ireland, but especially in Dublin. Among the major buildings erected during the eighteenth century were Parliament House, the Custom House and many private houses in the city and in

The River Liffey enters Dublin through a park and leaves it through the docks that line its exit to the sea. On the way it passes the fine Courts of Justice and the Custom House on the north bank, and Christ Church Cathedral, the castle and Trinity College, which are set back on the south bank, traditionally the smart side of the city.

the surrounding countryside; Powerscourt, Summerhill, Carton and others date from this time.

With its great natural beauty and its wealth of ancient buildings, Ireland, especially in the southern counties, has become a major tourist destination. Even with the annual influx of summer visitors, the roads are never crowded, nor does the tempo of life change its leisurely pace.

Around Dublin's Fair City

The capital of Ireland is an elegant city with many paradoxically down-to-earth and even inelegant corners, a combination which provides many exciting contrasts as the Dublin of Sheridan comes to terms with the Dublin of Brendan Behan. The city is almost encircled by two canals, the Royal to the north and the Grand to the south, both of which empty into the River Liffey. Most of the historic buildings are to be found in the southern part of the city, though the splendid Custom House, designed by James Gandon in the eighteenth century, lies along the north bank of the river. Also on the north bank is the impressive dome-topped building of the Four Courts which, like the Custom House, was almost destroyed in the civil war of the 1920s but later rebuilt.

Across O'Connell Bridge to the south is Trinity College, founded in 1591 on the site of a priory suppressed by Henry VIII and rebuilt in splendid style in the eighteenth century. The library contains some half million books, including such priceless manuscripts as the eighth-century illuminated Book of Kells. Dublin also has a University College, part of the National University of Ireland.

Behind and to the south of Trinity College are some of the best preserved Georgian houses for which Dublin is renowned and where many of the city's celebrities, such as the Duke of Wellington and W. B. Yeats, were born. Leinster House, the seat of the Irish Parliament, and the National Gallery are also in this area. To the south-west lies St. Stephen's Green, a pretty open space with lawns and trees surrounded by handsome Georgian houses and adorned by numerous busts and statues of Irish luminaries.

The medieval centre of Dublin was grouped round the castle, which was the centre of city life at the time of the Protestant Ascendancy. Later the building fell into decay and was used as a prison. In more recent times it was refurbished, and certain state rooms and St. Patrick's Hall, where Irish Presidents are inaugurated, are now open to visitors. However, almost nothing can be seen to indicate the castle's medieval grimness, as the present building is largely of the eighteenth century. Near the castle is the City Hall, built in 1769 as a Royal Exchange, and Christ Church Cathedral, where Lambert Simnel, then aged ten, and who claimed the throne of England through his alleged father, the Earl of Warwick, was crowned in 1487.

Another cathedral in this part of the city is St. Patrick's, where Jonathan Swift was dean from 1743 to 1745. Founded in 1180, though with a fourteenth-century tower, the cathedral was extensively rebuilt in the nineteenth century.

The River Liffey flows out of the capital into Dublin Bay, where the famous prawns come from. The bay is enclosed to the north by the Howth Peninsula, which has a popular resort, and to the south by Dun Laoghaire, a large resort town and terminal for the sea ferries from Holyhead, on Anglesey. Near Dun Laoghaire, at Sandycove Point, is the Martello tower included in *Ulysses* by James Joyce, who stayed in it for a short time. It is now a small museum.

The countryside around Dublin is rich in castles and manor houses. On Howth Peninsula is Howth Castle, which has beautiful rhododendron gardens surrounding the building, whose keep dates back to the mid-sixteenth century. To the west of Dublin, in Celbridge, is one of Ireland's finest Palladian mansions, Castletown House, designed for William Connolly, Speaker of the House of Commons, in 1722. The Italian architect Galilei was responsible for this superb house, flanked by two elegant colonnades.

Another fine mansion, Powerscourt House, unfortunately gutted by fire in 1974, lies in the hills west of Bray near Enniskerry. The house, which is privately owned, is not open to the public, but the gardens and estate offer a superb example of landscaping in the grand manner.

Right: Powerscourt is a vast 14,000-acre (5666-hectare) estate in County Wicklow and, though the house was damaged by fire in 1974, remains one of the great demesnes of Ireland. The superb park has ornamental lakes, a waterfall and statuary, and is well wooded.

The Eastern Coastlands

Ireland has 3,000 miles (over 4 800 km) of strongly indented coastline, so that nowhere, however far inland, is more than 70 miles (113 km) from the sea. In the west, where it is met by the force of the Atlantic, the coast is rugged, but on the eastern seaboard it is characterized by long, gently sloping beaches washed by relatively shallow seas.

Along the north-east coast, in County Antrim, one of the counties of Ulster, the land does drop steeply to the sea, and looks across a 13-mile (21-km) channel of sea to Scotland. There are steamer ferries from Cairnryan and Stranraer to Larne and air services to bring visitors to one of the best of the many lovely coast roads of Ireland. Inland lie Lough Neagh, the largest lake in the British Isles, and the Bann valley, set in a land of rolling uplands that contrast with the splendid coast of Antrim, with its steep headlands backed by the outlines of the mountains inland. To the south is Belfast, originally a stronghold of the O'Neills, who held it against Scottish and English incursions for over 300 years until the sixteenth century, when it was taken over by the governor of Carrickfergus. His fine castle still stands. The eighteenth and nineteenth centuries were a period of economic and cultural development in Belfast, and many of the buildings of interest today date from this period.

Overleaf: Some of the prettiest scenery of the east coast of Ireland is to be found in County Louth, to the south of Carlingford Lough. The Mountains of Mourne rise steeply to the north of the lough and the Cooley Hills to the south. Carlingford town itself is on the southern bank of the lough at the foot of Slieve Foye (1,935 feet/590 m).

To the south of Belfast, in County Down, are the celebrated Mountains of Mourne, whose granite mass rises to 2,796 feet (852 m) at Slieve Donard, in strong contrast to the low, heavily cultivated hills which characterize the rest of this green, fertile county. Kilkeel, a fishing port, is a popular centre for visits to the mountains, the Neolithic remains to the south-west and the Norman castle which guards the entrance to Carlingford Lough, a steep-sided sea inlet some ten miles (16 km) long also to the south-west.

Castles are plentiful in the area, for Louth, which appears again and again in the epics of ancient Ireland, was a disputed territory for centuries, first with the Danes and later with the English, a fact not easy to recall today as one admires its gently undulating and fertile countryside and the wide, sandy bays, cut by the occasional rocky headland, of its coast. Drogheda, on the River Boyne estuary, was another even more important strategic town controlling entry from the sea as well as the river crossing. In medieval times it was a walled fortified town, but little remains of these fortifications today except St. Lawrence's Gate, one of the best examples of fortified town gates in Ireland.

Monasterboice, in the south of Louth in the Boyne valley on the borders of County Meath, is a quiet place notable for the ruins of a monastic community founded by St. Buithe towards the end of the fifth century. Today the visitor can see two churches, one of them 1,100 years old, and a round tower. There is also an exceptionally fine example of an early-Christian high cross, called Muiredach's Cross, near the entrance to the graveyard. To the west lies Mellifont Abbey, the first Cistercian monastery in Ireland, founded in 1142 and now a ruin.

Farther west the Boyne, which is a salmon-fishing river, is joined by the Blackwater, another fine fishing river, at Navan, to the south of which is the Hill of Tara, the religious centre of ancient Ireland. It was here that the tribes of pre-Christian Ireland met and where disputes between them were settled in those early days of Irish history. On the top of the hill is a stone said to be the coronation stone of the Irish kings.

Along the Blackwater lies Kells, County Meath, where the famous illuminated book of the Gospels was created in the ninth century, though some believe it was brought from Iona. The original is at Trinity College, Dublin, but a facsimile is held at St. Columba's Church in Kells. The house of St. Colmcille (or Columba), the founder of the monastic order that produced the Book of Kells, is in the town, and there is a fine example of the round towers, found all over Ireland, which served as storehouses and refuges in time of trouble.

To the south, but still on the River Boyne which rises far to the south in County Kildare, Trim Castle, the largest Anglo-Norman stronghold in Ireland, stands proudly on its grassy mound in the centre of Trim, in the strategically important country north-west of Dublin.

Kildare, with its lush pastures and spreading grasslands, is a focus for the Irish love of horse-racing. Famous Irish classic races are run at the Curragh, while Punchestown, near Naas, is a fashionable venue for point-to-point meetings.

The country to the south of the River Boyne is hilly, the chief range being the Wicklow Mountains, which run parallel to the coast as far as County Wexford. Called the 'Garden of Ireland', Wicklow's varied scenery ranges from the gentle farmland of the central plain and the grandeur of the steep glens and heavily wooded valleys of the mountains to the low, sandy sweeps of the eastern coastline. One of the highest points of the former military road through Wicklow is at Mount Djouce (2,358 feet/729 m), from where the road traverses a wild and bleak moorland until it descends into the beautiful valleys of Glenmacnass and Glendalough, both in County Wicklow and among the most-photographed beauty spots in Ireland. There are two lakes at Glendalough, surrounded by wooded mountains whose rocky outcrops attract climbers and hill walkers. Glendalough is only 18 miles (29 km) from the coast at Arklow, via the lovely Avonmore valley, where Charles Parnell lived, and the Vale of Avoca. Arklow, attractively sited at the mouth of the River Avoca, is one of the many excellent seaside resorts along the east coast of Ireland, but it is also a port where fishing, shipping and shipbuilding have been going on for centuries. Sir Francis Chichester's *Gipsy Moth III* was built here. Farther north is Wicklow, the county town, which is also a seaside resort. Nearer to Dublin is Bray, the largest and

Muiredach's Cross at Monasterboice, County Louth, is a fine example of an early Christian monolith. It stands in the graveyard of the ancient abbey founded by St. Buithe and was probably made for Muiredach, the abbot of Monasterboice.

longest-established resort on the east coast, which is crowded at summer weekends with Dubliners looking for relaxation and entertainment.

The most southerly town of the east coast is Wexford, an old town with winding streets, probably best known today for its annual opera festival in October. During the summer season Wexford attracts many sailing enthusiasts. At Wexford, the River Slaney, flowing down from the Wicklow Mountains, enters Wexford harbour, which is usually busy with the fishing boats that moor along the quaysides. Only one of the five fortified gateways which once protected Wexford are still standing, but there are many other ancient remains to interest visitors.

To the north of Wexford is Enniscorthy, with its important Norman castle in which the poet Edmund Spenser lived. Rosslare, the port for ferries from Fishguard in Wales and from France, lies to the south of Wexford.

The Coast and Rivers of the South-East

In southern Ireland between Wexford and the city of Cork the rivers flow south into the Celtic Sea, carving out valleys, some gentle and some deep, through the hills and mountains. Much of this land is in the County of Waterford, whose splendid mountains, soft and gentle valleys and hills, and rugged coastline combine to create unrivalled scenic loveliness.

In the east, the River Slaney flows down from the Wicklow Mountains to Wexford, and in the west the Blackwater, rising on the borders of Kerry, flows eastward through some of the loveliest river scenery in all Ireland to Youghal. In between are the Suir and the Nore, with its important tributary the Barrow, all providing corridors of communication to central Ireland and, in the past, an obstacle to invaders travelling from the east. Along the river valleys there is a wealth of towns, castles and abbeys of great antiquity set in a countryside of pleasant landscapes.

One of these towns is New Ross, built on a hillside overlooking the River Barrow. Despite its name, New Ross is one of the oldest towns in Wexford and

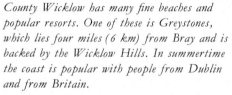

County Wicklow has many fine beaches and popular resorts. One of these is Greystones, which lies four miles (6 km) from Bray and is backed by the Wicklow Hills. In summertime the coast is popular with people from Dublin and from Britain.

was probably the site of a sixth-century monastery now buried under the thirteenth-century St. Mary's Abbey. Near New Ross is Dunganstown, the village home of the great-great-grandfather of President John Kennedy, while to the south are the extensive ruins of Dunbrody Abbey.

In its upper reaches, the River Barrow passes through the town of Carlow, an old Anglo-Norman town which, because it stood on the borders of the English Pale, the district centred on Dublin under English control, was at one time an embattled frontier post. One wall and two towers of the old castle still stand. Upriver from Carlow at Athy, County Kildare's largest town, is another castle, White's Castle, strategically placed to control the passage across the river.

The River Nore, into which the Barrow flows just above New Ross, is equally well endowed with castles at strategic crossings, and the broad rich valley of the river also attracted the founders of monasteries. Near Thomastown, whose castle was taken by Cromwell, are the impressive ruins of Jerpoint Abbey.

Upstream, the Nore flows through Kilkenny, county town of the sporting county of Kilkenny and the seat of many of the early parliaments of the

County Carlow is a very small inland county between County Kildare and County Wicklow. The River Barrow flows south through it past Carlow town and the Black Castle at Leighlinbridge, which saw much of the conflict that took place on the borders of the English Pale, the occupied area around Dublin.

233

Kilmore Quay, in County Wexford, is a secluded coastal village with white stone houses roofed with thatch. From the village one can visit the Saltee Islands, Ireland's largest bird sanctuary. Kilmore is a popular centre of sea angling.

fourteenth century. For six brief but glorious years in the 1640s the Confederation of Kilkenny functioned here. Kilkenny Castle stands on the high bank of the River Nore at the south-east end of the city and is a powerful-looking thirteenth-century stronghold. The Dukes of Ormonde once ruled the surrounding land from this fortress, but today the castle belongs to the state. Farther north, in the inland county of Laoise, the Nore passes the elegant home of the Viscount de Vesci, Abbeyleix, which is open to the public in summer and is a fine example of the type of mansion built during the more peaceful periods of Irish history.

The Rivers Nore and Suir both reach the sea near the city of Waterford, where they enter the long and sheltered Waterford estuary, in which there is a constant coming and going of ships and pleasure craft. The city, on the banks of the Suir, is one of the busiest ports of southern Ireland, shipping out furniture, iron-foundry products, meat and Waterford glass, which has been manufactured here since the eighteenth century. One of the oldest buildings in the city is Reginald's Tower, a cylindrical structure on the quayside built in the eleventh century as part of the city's defences against the Danes.

Like the Nore, the River Suir offers a good route along its valley into the inland countryside of Waterford and to Tipperary, Ireland's biggest inland county. In its course through Tipperary, the Suir runs from north to south across a broad plain, whose fertile soil, extending west into Limerick, has earned it the name of the Golden Vale. Near its southern extremity, where the river turns east before cutting through the mountains to Carrick-on-Suir and the south coast, is

Clonmel. This is the chief town of County Tipperary and it has much that is of interest, including a substantial part of the old town wall which now partly encloses St. Mary's Church.

At Cahir, upstream, there is a castle which once dominated the intersection of the roads from Dublin to Cork and from Limerick to Waterford. Cahir, like Cashel to the north, was a headquarters for the kings of Munster, who first had their place of coronation at the Motte of Knockgraffon four miles (6 km) north of Cahir and later at Cashel on the famous Rock. This strange limestone outcrop in the centre of the plain was the seat of Munster kings for more than 700 years, from 370 until 1101, and was the spot where St. Patrick baptized the kings of his time. The Rock was ceded to the Church in the twelfth century and a cathedral was built upon it. The present dramatic ruins date from a later period, however, and comprise a ruined cathedral, the fifteenth-century Hall of the Vicars Choral, and Cormac's Chapel. The latter is of special interest for its high-pitched corbelled roof and the tympanum with a carving of a large beast struggling with a centaur. Near the base of the rock is a Dominican friary founded in the thirteenth century.

Tipperary, to the west of Cashel, was founded in the twelfth century and grew in importance during the Anglo-Norman period. Later it was sacked and burned by the O'Briens and remained a ruin for many years. Today it is a market town, the centre of the dairy-farming industry that flourishes in the fertile meadows of the Golden Vale, and there are only meagre remains of its ancient castle and abbey.

The seat of the Munster kings at Cashel, County Tipperary, is one of the great sights of Ireland. Around the Rock and its ruins are other interesting buildings, among which are Hore Abbey, built in 1266, and Longfield House, five miles (8 km) to the north.

The Wild South-West

For many people, the jagged coast of the south-west of Ireland is without equal.
This is the coast of the counties of Cork, Ireland's largest, and Kerry, split by its
three great peninsulas thrusting out into the Atlantic. On this coast are
mountains that face the challenge of Atlantic weather and rocks battered by its
waves. Wild rocky headlands, sandy coves, solitary islands and wooded shores
merge to provide a romantic landscape that has combined with the Irish soul to
create a legendary world.

Cork, on the edge of the great south-western coast, is Ireland's third largest
city, and its large and sheltered harbour is an export centre for the products of
local industry and southern agriculture. Many of Cork's fine buildings, including
the City Hall, the Court House and the University College, were built in the
nineteenth century. Near the city centre is Shandon Church, an eighteenth-century
building with an impressive multicoloured tower, from which there are
panoramic views over the city. Another building of the same period is the
Church of Ireland Cathedral of St. Finbarre, below which, it is believed, lie the
foundations of the sixth-century church built by the saint himself alongside the
south channel of the River Lee.

Five miles (8 km) north-east of Cork is famous Blarney Castle, where
thousands have leaned perilously backwards over the parapet to kiss the famous
Blarney Stone, which is traditionally supposed to confer the gift of eloquence.
From Blarney, a road leads north to Mallow and Limerick, which lies in the
broad plain that borders the River Shannon; this road is a kind of frontier
between the mountainous country to the west and the blander landscapes of the
east. In this region are sixteenth-century Kanturk Castle, on a tributary of
the Blackwater River, Muckross House and Muckross Abbey, the ruin of a lovely
fifteenth-century abbey set in its glorious 11,000-acre (4,452-hectare) park, and, of
course, there is Killarney itself, the glory of inland Kerry. Nearly 20,000 acres
(8,094 hectares) of wild woodland and mountains surround the romantically
beautiful lakes which attract thousands of visitors every year to the lovely valley,

set between mountains and purple heather-covered hills. Ladies' View is one of the best places from which to see Killarney, for it offers a breathtaking panorama of the island-studded lakes, the wooded hills and the mountain glens of this particularly lovely part of Ireland.

Despite Killarney, it is still the coast that is the major attraction for visitors from all over the world. South of Cork, down on the attractive estuary of the River Bandon which cuts into the rugged coastline, is Kinsale, a delightful fishing harbour and seaside resort, with a splendid headland to the west topped by a ruined watchtower, from which sentries once looked out to sea waiting for Napoleon's ships. There is some superb cliff-walking country along here to Clonakilty and Skibbereen, north-west of which lies the wonderful, deep inlet of Bantry Bay, unfortunately spoiled at Bantry, at its head, by the oil-storage tanks at Whiddy Island.

On the north side of the bay is Glengarriff, a small resort that spreads over a wooded valley opening out into a bay full of islands rich in trees and shrubbery. Glengarriff lies at the eastern end of the Beara Peninsula, a scenic finger of land shared by Cork and Kerry, along which run the Caha Mountains. The 1,887-foot (575-m) Sugarloaf Mountain rises at the eastern end of the exciting Healy Pass, which runs to the north at Ardigole Bridge, flanked on the west by Hungry Hill. Castletown, where the road winds round to the northern side of Beara, is a popular resort.

The northern shore of the Beara Peninsula gives some lovely views across the water to the Ring of Kerry on the Iveragh Peninsula, and leads to Kenmare at the eastern end of the broad Kenmare estuary. Kenmare is a well-patronized resort and is an excellent entry point to the country of the Killarney lakes. The road north is flanked by Macgillicuddy's Reeks, some of Ireland's highest mountains, rising to 3,414 feet (1041 m) at Carrantuohill.

The Ring of Kerry road starts from Kenmare and skirts 75 miles (121 km) of coastline right round the Iveragh Peninsula. The drive offers scenery of exceptional beauty combining land and sea in wonderful vistas, and is an essential tour for anyone visiting the west of Ireland. As one leaves Kenmare, Dunkerron

From Aghadoe Hill on the east bank there is a fine view of Lough Leane, one of the beautiful lakes of Killarney. On the hill are the ruins of a round tower and church, and a short walk away is Ross Castle, a well-preserved ruin dating back to the fourteenth century.

Castle can be seen to the south, and the island-studded estuary of the Kenmare River beyond. The road then passes through Parknasilla and Sneem, which has pretty houses painted in bright colours, and rounds a headland into Ballinskelligs Bay. The Skellig rocks are out to sea and can be reached by boat from Waterville on the bay, but only when the sea is calm. There is an early Irish monastery on one of the rocks. Waterville is built on a piece of land separating Ballinskelligs Bay from beautiful Lough Currane, a lake with numerous islands and the western peaks of the Macgillicuddy's Reeks rising impressively around it. The whole area is rich in prehistoric stone and ancient forts built before the Christian era.

From Cahirciveen along the north coast of the peninsula the Ring of Kerry is at its finest, offering panoramic views across to the Dingle Peninsula, the most northerly of Kerry's three great peninsulas. The town of Dingle, an important port in Tudor times and now a pleasant town and touring centre, lies halfway along the southern edge of the peninsula, which rivals the Ring of Kerry for its wild and remote mountainous beauty.

Tralee, on the north-east side of the peninsula is on a plain where the River Lee enters Tralee Bay, and a particularly fine route to it from Dingle crosses the peninsula north-eastwards via the Connor Pass between the Brandon and central Dingle mountains. A few remains of the castle of the Desmond family can be seen in Tralee, which is Kerry's main town and famous for the song 'The Rose of Tralee' by William Mulchinok who lived nearby at Ballymullen.

Around Kerry Head on Kerry's north-west coast, lies Ballybullion, a popular resort set on a rugged coastline of cliffs, caves, small coves and pleasant beaches. The town lies on the southern shore of the great mouth of the Shannon, where Ireland's rugged south-west region meets its far west.

Ireland's Western Lands

The River Shannon, flowing down from Ireland's lake-filled centre, provides a natural border for the west country, which encompasses counties whose names seem to spring from the country's history, especially her literary history: Limerick and Clare, Galway, Mayo, Roscommon, Sligo, Leitrim and Donegal.

In the south, especially in Limerick, much of the land is low-lying and undulating, and marked by fertile farmlands, though there are fringes of hills to add variety to the scenery. The town of Limerick, on the estuary of the Shannon, was a walled town until the eighteenth century, when the walls were removed. Because of its strategic importance at the mouth of the Shannon, the town was a much coveted prize in the early days of Irish history.

Among Limerick's most interesting buildings are the castle, built by King John to guard the Shannon river-crossing, St. Mary's Cathedral, which includes some of the remains of an O'Brien palace, and the Catholic church of St. John with its 280-foot (85-m) tower. On the north side of the Shannon is Shannon International Airport, which has brought wealth as well as noise to this part of County Clare. It has also stimulated the tourist industry, especially in attractions like Bunratty Castle, once the home of the O'Briens of Thomond, where medieval banquets take place for the entertainment of passing travellers. There is also the Bunratty Folk Park, where traditional Irish dancing and singing are performed among the reconstructed cottages brought to the site from various parts of Ireland.

As one travels west, County Clare changes in character, becoming denuded of trees by the Atlantic gales and with a meagre and rocky terrain that does not encourage farming. Nevertheless, Clare has a wild beauty that is particularly noticeable along the coast. The high spot, in more ways than one, is at the cliffs of Moher which tower some 700 feet (213 m) above the sea. From their commanding height one can see the Aran Islands to the north-west.

The islands, lying 30 miles (48 km) out to sea from the city of Galway, are inhabited by fishermen and their families. They were a major inspiration of the poet-playwright J. M. Synge, whose play *Riders to the Sea* is set in the islands. There are three islands, Inishmore, Inishmaan and Inisheer, and they are all equally wild and barren. Nevertheless, people have lived here since pre-Christian times, as is evident from the stone forts, such as the strongly walled Duns

Right: Garinish Island lies off the north bank of the Kenmare River near Sneem. The island is the property of the Earl of Dunraven and has beautiful gardens, part of which are laid out in the Italian style. The sandy coves of the island are gathering places of the Atlantic seal.

Overleaf: Castletownbere is a fishing port at the western end of Bantry Bay. Bear Island protects the entrance to the harbour and Dunboy Castle, the seat of the Sullivan O'Beres, is nearby.

Aengus on Inishmore, and other antiquities found in the islands. Today the small white cottages, set amid small fields surrounded by stone walls, have themselves something of the look of forts, though their protection is against the intemperate weather and not Viking invaders.

The Aran Islands lie at the entrance to Galway Bay, at the eastern end of which Galway, the principal city of County Galway, is situated. The city lies on the narrow neck of land between the bay and Lough Corrib, a lake which divides the county into two contrasting areas. To the west is the scenically awe-inspiring land of Connemara, where the Twelve Pins, or Twelve Bens, mountain range dominates the horizons, and to the east is a fertile plain extending to Roscommon and the Shannon.

In the isolated lands of Connemara Irish is still spoken and the Gaelic culture is preserved. This is a wild and sparsely inhabited landscape whose rich colours – brown, purple and many shades of green – have inspired painters. The inland hills rise to their highest point (2,395 feet/730 m) in the Twelve Bens near Clifden, the largest resort town in Connemara.

The loughs that lie between the western and eastern lands of Galway and Mayo are Lough Corrib to the south, Lough Mask and Lough Conn to the north. The largest is Corrib, from which the River Corrib flows down to Galway city. To the north of Lough Mask is another small lake, Lough Carra, at the northern end of which is Ballintubber Abbey, once owned by the Moore family, but now considerably restored and open to the public. Not far away, Castlebar, the county town of Mayo, lies in the centre of a limestone plain. The road westward from here leads to the coast and to the marvellous Mayo coastline of beaches, headlands, cliffs and islands, including Achill Island, the largest island off Ireland's coast, to which it is connected by bridge. Mayo's coast also has several attractive resorts. To the north is Bellmullet, almost an island surrounded by Blacksod Bay, Broad Haven and the Atlantic Ocean; the isthmus that joins it to the mainland has a natural defence, and a castle with a 200-foot-long (61-m) wall was built across it at Dunamoo Point.

The Dingle Peninsula, in County Kerry, is famed for its impressive coastal scenery. Dingle, the most important seaport on the peninsula, lies on Dingle Harbour under the green slopes of Brandon Mountain (3,127 feet/953 m). In Elizabethan times Dingle was an important walled trading port.

Kylemore Abbey is in Connemara, County
Galway, amid beautiful mountain scenery. The
road which circles the peaks of the Twelve Pins
of Connemara runs through Kylemore.

Inland from Bellmullet, due east to Ballina, Mayo's largest town, runs a fine
coastal road with superb scenery all the way. From here, too, the Irish coastline
dips eastward along the shores of Sligo and Leitrim. Sligo, though a small
county, can offer fine and varied scenery for, while the coast is largely flat and
low-lying, there are mountains inland. Near Sligo town, which has the ruin of a
Dominican abbey is Lough Gill with its Isle of Innisfree, immortalized by the
poet W. B. Yeats.

To the north lies Donegal, the most northerly county of Ireland, and one
whose beauty, made up of a heavily indented coastline, glens, lakes and
mountains, is outstanding even among the other beautiful coasts of the west.
Donegal is sparsely populated, the many invaders of Irish territory never having
thought it rich enough to fight over, and though there are few of the strongholds
and abbeys one finds in the south-west and east, there are many other historic
sites and antiquities to be seen.

Donegal town, tucked away in a corner of Donegal Bay, does have a ruined
castle, however, standing on the banks of the River Eske. It belonged to the
O'Donnells, and one of its interesting features today is a fine Jacobean wing
attached to the massive gabled and turreted tower. Another castle, at Creeslough
at the northern extreme of Donegal, is Doe Castle, which was built by the

Above: Benbulben, in County Sligo on the road from Sligo to Bundoran, is a steep, flat-topped mountain 1,730 feet (527 m) high. It has often featured in Irish poetry, and the poet W. B. Yeats is buried within sight of it at Drumcliff.

Left: Achill Island, the largest Irish offshore island, is joined to the mainland by a bridge. The island is mountainous, rising to 2,204 feet (672 m) at Slieve More in the south, and has an attractive resort at Keel, where cliffs drop 800 feet (244 m) to the sea and there is a long, sandy beach.

MacSweeneys in the sixteenth century and was fought over by various tribal chiefs of the north, many of whom are buried in the adjoining graveyard, once a monastery.

To the east of Doe Castle is Lough Swilly, where the sea penetrates deeply southwards and which, with Lough Foyle farther east, isolates the Inishowen Peninsula and Malin Head, Ireland's most northerly point. The peninsula is a mountainous region, with its highest point at 2,019-foot (615-m) Slieve Snacht. There are various seaside resorts along its coasts and one of the oldest relics of northern Ireland, the Crianan of Aileach, a stone fort built around 1700 BC which overlooks the countryside of Lough Swilly and Lough Foyle and as far as Londonderry on the River Foyle.

Londonderry is an ancient town whose houses are built on a steep hill above the river. St. Columba founded a monastery here in the sixth century and the town was frequently attacked by the Danes until the eleventh century; after that it was constantly at war with the Anglo-Normans, finally being occupied by the English in the sixteenth century. Today one can walk along the old town walls, on which some of the cannon that once defended the town still stand, but there are few old buildings left other than St. Columba's cathedral, dating from the seventeenth century, and the Catholic church of the same name and period.

On the coast to the east of Derry, and beyond the long sweep of Magilligan strand and the resorts of Portstewart and Portrush, is perhaps the most famous natural phenomenon in all Ireland. This is the Giant's Causeway, at Benbane

Head in County Antrim. The extraordinary terraces of prism-shaped basalt columns, which are the result of volcanic action, have been an attraction for tourists since the nineteenth century. Visits to the Causeway are well organized, with guides to point out the various sections, which have been given fanciful names such as the Giant's Horseshoe and the Lady's Fan.

At the north-east extremity of Ireland is Torr Head, a mere 13 miles (21 km) from the Mull of Kintyre in Scotland.

The Lakes of Ireland

The centre of Ireland is a flat land of rivers and lakes – 800 in all – with the great waterway of the River Shannon rising in the north on Cuilcagh Mountain in County Cavan and, having flowed through a string of lakes, ending at the Shannon estuary between Limerick and County Clare. This beautiful waterway is navigable for 140 miles (225 km) from Lough Key in the north to Killaloe north of Limerick.

At its northern end, the Shannon flows through the country that lies north-east of Lough Allen and then, leaving the lake, passes through Carrick-on-Shannon, the county town of Leitrim, which is a popular boating and fishing centre. Flowing south, the river passes through small Lough Bofin and arrives at Lanesborough, in County Longford at the entrance to Lough Ree. The land is low-lying and green here, with farms and bogs. To the east is Longford town, lying on the Kamlin River, which flows into the Shannon, and to the west is Roscommon, a resort with many outdoor sports amenities. Roscommon has the ruins of a Dominican abbey founded in the thirteenth century by the king of Connacht and a castle built in the same century by the Lord Chief Justice of Ireland. The castle was surrendered to Cromwell's forces in 1652.

Below Lough Ree the Shannon flows through Athlone, a resort from which visitors explore the shores and islands of the lough, many of which have the remains of ancient churches. This is known as Poet's Country for Oliver Goldsmith and John Keegan Casey were born near Athlone.

Left: Slieve League (1,972 feet/601 m), in the south of County Donegal, is only accessible on foot from Malinbeg. The dramatic south face drops away to the sea. Killybegs, one of Ireland's most important fishing ports, lies to the east.

Preceding pages: There is some fine scenery along Teelin Bay in County Donegal. Nearby, over Carrigan Head, a track leads to lonely Lough O'Mulligan and the Bunglass Cliffs, which rise 1,024 feet (312 m) above the sea.

At Portumna, a fishing centre, the Shannon enters Lough Derg, the last lough before reaching the sea. This is the largest lake on the Shannon's course and a beautiful one, especially in the Scarriff inlet on the County Clare shore. The western shore is in Tipperary, where the most important town, Nenagh, has a fine castle and keep. South of Nenagh lie the Silvermine Mountains where silver was extracted for many years. Remains of a Kennedy castle can be seen near Silvermines village.

Leaving Lough Derg, the Shannon passes through Killaloe, now a boating centre for Lough Derg, and to the west of which lie the Slieve Bernagh mountains. Killaloe has a cathedral which was built in the twelfth century but restored in the eighteenth. In the cathedral can be seen a Romanesque doorway said to have been the entrance to the tomb of Murtagh O'Brien, king of Munster, who died in 1120. Below Killaloe is the fort of Beal Boru, meaning 'pass of the tributes', near which Brian Boru had his palace at Kincora.

To the east of the Shannon lies a maze of lakes and waterways which run from Lough Erne in the north to Lough Owel near Mullingar in West Meath County. Lough Erne consists of two large lakes, the Upper and Lower Lough Erne.

Portrush, in County Antrim, is situated on the promontory of Ramore Head, which provides fine views. The town is a popular resort and is within easy reach of the Giant's Causeway and its strange rock formations of basalt columns.

Overleaf: Enniskillen Castle, in County Fermanagh, has been largely rebuilt, but its turreted gateway dates back to the seventeenth century. The castle, which stands by the river between Upper and Lower Lough Erne, is now the county museum.

Lough Tay, one of Ireland's many beautiful lakes, lies in the lovely Wicklow mountains of County Wicklow near Roundwood. This area of wooded hills is a playground for Dubliners and overseas visitors alike.

Enniskillen lies at the southern end of the Lower Lough between the two lakes, and is a centre at which many boats of all kinds are hired to visitors who want to explore the lake. Enniskillen Castle, now a museum, stands guard over the area along the River Erne, which flows north to Donegal Bay. In the Lower Lough, Devenish Island contains some interesting religious buildings, including a round tower 85 feet (26 m) high.

To the south, farther up the River Erne in the lowland part of County Cavan, there are more small lakes, including Lough Oughter. In the centre of the lake is Cloughoughter Castle, an O'Reilly stronghold of the thirteenth century. Cavan, the county town, lies to the east. Farther south are Lough Gowna, Lough Sheelin and others which form part of the great network of lakes and rivers which cross this part of Ireland, in which stretches of water are rarely out of sight.

Index

(Figures in italic type refer to illustrations)